KARMIC PALMISTRY

ABOUT THE AUTHOR

When he was six years old, Jon Saint-Germain learned to read palms from his grandmother. He has been a lifelong student of the craft ever since. Jon has been a professional psychic entertainer and palm reader for over twenty years. He is a popular lecturer on palmistry, and his show "MindBenders" takes him across the country. Jon has written thirteen books on psychic subjects and the psychology of entertainment. In 1997, he was awarded the Blackwood Award by the Psychic Entertainer's Association for his contributions to the literatures of mentalism. He lives in Knoxville, Tennessee, with his wife, Elizabeth, and three cats, Oliver, Boo, and Emma.

Explore Past Lives, Soul Mates, & Karma

KARMIC PALMISTRY

JON SAINT-GERMAIN

Foreword by Richard Webster

2003
Llewellyn Publications
St. Paul, Minnesota 55164-0383, U.S.A.

First Edition
First Printing, 2003

Book design and editing by Joanna Willis
Cover design by Lisa Novak
Cover image © 2002 by Shirley Huller-White
Interior illustrations by Llewellyn art department

Library of Congress Cataloging-in-Publication Data
Saint-Germain, Jon, 1960–
   Karmic palmistry: explore past lives, soul mates & karma/Jon Saint-Germain; foreword by Richard Webster.—1st ed.
     p.   cm.
   Includes bibliographical references and index.
   ISBN 0-7287-0317-6
    1. Palmistry. 2. Karma. I. Title.

BF921.S215 2003
133.6—dc21

                                                             2002043479

Llewellyn Worldwide does not participate in, endorse, or have any authority or responsibility concerning private business transactions between our authors and the public.

   All mail addressed to the author is forwarded but the publisher cannot, unless specifically instructed by the author, give out an address or phone number.

   Any Internet references contained in this work are current at publication time, but the publisher cannot guarantee that a specific location will continue to be maintained. Please refer to the publisher's website for links to authors' websites and other sources.

Llewellyn Publications
A Division of Llewellyn Worldwide, Ltd.
P.O. Box 64383, Dept. 0-7387-0317-6
St. Paul, MN 55164-0383, U.S.A.
www.llewellyn.com

 Printed in the United States of America on recycled paper

ALSO BY JON SAINT-GERMAIN

Runic Palmistry

To my cat Checkers,
who taught me that death
is never the end.

CONTENTS

FOREWORD

$\mathcal{I}$ spent two very happy years in London in the late 1960s. Palmistry was extremely popular there at the time, and I learned a great deal from my contacts with other palmists and members of a chirological society to which I belonged. I was busy, as I worked in publishing during the day and read palms in my spare time. A number of the professional palmists I met in London were from India, including a remarkable man named Mir Bashir. He was the author of a small book on palmistry called *How to Read Hands*, and he also conducted classes and workshops on the subject. When I first met him, he had just started writing what was to become his major work, *The Art of Hand Analysis*. He was also the first person I met who knew anything about the karmic aspects of palmistry.

Mir Bashir had achieved a degree of fame in India for his predictions. He had successfully prophesied India's independence, the emancipation of women, and the division between India and Pakistan. He also predicted the problems that would ensue as a result. He moved to London in 1947 and quickly established a busy practice as a consultant palmist. Mir Bashir, and a small group of other talented palmists, were responsible for the popularity that palmistry was enjoying when I arrived in London. They were carrying on a tradition of British palmistry that began with Cheiro and continued with the work and researches of Katharine

St. Hill, Noel Jaquin, Henry Frith, Charlotte Wolff, Fred Gettings, Beryl Hutchinson, and many others.

The friendship and support of the Indian palmists I met in London made me decide to visit India. Armed with a few letters of introduction, I arrived in Bombay in April 1969. I was expecting to learn a great deal from the palmists in India. After all, it was supposed to be the spiritual home of palmistry. Unfortunately, I quickly discovered that most of the palmists I met had learned the subject from Western authors, such as William Benham. I arrived there expecting to learn, but most of the time found myself teaching more than learning.

Fortunately, I ultimately found a handful of dedicated palm readers who introduced me to a study of the minor lines of the hand, different methods of hand classification, interesting techniques for timing events, and karmic factors.

It is not surprising that karma plays such an important role in Indian palmistry. After all, reincarnation is accepted by almost everyone there. They believe that if they lead a good life in this incarnation, they will be reborn into better circumstances in their next lifetime. Consequently, the belief that a good deed done today will bear fruit later on (even possibly in the next incarnation) ensures that most people actively try to lead good, rather than bad, lives. Obviously, the concept of karma means that bad deeds need to be repaid at a later date also. Karma is completely impartial, and follows the law of cause and effect. As the Bible says, "As ye sow, so shall ye reap."

My happiest memories of India in the late 1960s revolve around the many pleasant late-night conversations I had with a small group of palmists in New Delhi. We talked for hours about every aspect of palmistry, and always, sooner or later, the conversation would come back to karma and how it could be interpreted in the palms of the hands.

Much of this conversation revolved around the amount of control people had over their own destinies. Obviously, if someone had done terrible things in a previous life, he or she would be born with a huge karmic debt that would need to be repaid. Not many people had the necessary strength of character to repay this inherited karma. Consequently, an important part of a good palmist's job was to encourage clients to work hard at paying off their karmic debts. Sadly, only a small number of people are prepared to tackle this Herculean task before progressing with their lives. This means that most people are fated to lead limited and difficult lives because their karmic debts are not repaid.

In India, as in the West, it is common for people to say, "It's my karma," and feel that nothing can be done about it. No matter how bad the situation, there is always something that can be done. The palmists I met in New Delhi encouraged their clients to maintain a positive attitude and to express their love to everyone as positive steps to help overcome their karma. Our actions in the past dictate the karmic situation we are born into in this lifetime, but they have nothing to do with our response to it. We can sit back, moan about our fate, and do nothing, or we can consciously strive to repay the karma and then start to make considerable progress in this incarnation.

The attention paid to karma by good Eastern palmists is one of the major differences between Eastern and Western palmistry. In the West, most people consider palmistry to be nothing more than a form of fortune-telling. I have even met a few professional palmists who consider the art to be little more than that. In the East, the fortune-telling aspect is important, too, but the shape and markings on the hands are also interpreted to reveal the client's character, personality, potential, karma, and soul.

It is more than thirty years since I was introduced to Indian palmistry, and every now and again over the years I wondered why there were no books on karmic palmistry. After all, many books have been written on karmic astrology since Alan Leo introduced the subject to the West more than one hundred years ago. Happily, I no longer need concern myself about this, as my friend Jon Saint-Germain has accepted the challenge and written an excellent introduction to karmic palmistry. I especially like the fact that his book is easy to read, and contains many interesting anecdotes. A lesser writer would have written a dull and technical work on this subject, but Jon's book is both entertaining and highly informative.

This book will be of enormous benefit to anyone remotely interested in palmistry and karma. Professional palmists will learn a great deal from it, and people who have never read anything on the subject of palmistry before will also be able to follow and understand it. It would be hard to imagine a better introduction to this important subject.

Jon is not only an excellent writer, he is also a highly successful professional palmist with a busy practice. Everything in his book has been thoroughly tested with his clients. It may not be possible for you to ever have a reading with Jon, but with the help of his book, you will learn much more about yourself. Once you discover the karmic factors in your hands and act on them, your life will become smoother, easier, happier, and much more fulfilling.

RICHARD WEBSTER

INTRODUCTION

*From the very earliest times the study of the
hand has excited man's curiosity and stimu-
lated his imagination. Into the pattern of the
lines on his palm he has projected the course
of his destiny.*

—Charlotte Wolff, *The Human Hand*

One of the great things about being a student of palmistry is that the learning never ends. Just as no two people are exactly alike, no two hands are either, and the lessons found in the palms are endless. I must admit that quite often I learn more from my clients than they do from me!

Everyone is different, but we all have one thing in common. Rich or poor, beautiful or plain, famous or relatively unknown, we all struggle with the puzzling nature of life. "Why is life so hard?" we ask. "Why do bad things have to happen to me?" Sometimes we feel that our efforts go unnoticed and unrewarded. Other times we feel a vague sense of unhappiness; a restless feeling or deep dissatisfaction with our lives. "I know that I want *something*," we say, "but I don't know exactly what it is." When confronted with a mystery, intelligent people look for a solution. When the mystery concerns ourselves, we try to solve it with the help of those who peer into the mind and psyche of the human animal: psychologists, counselors, and psychics. We want information.

This is where palmistry, the art of reading hands, comes into the picture.

Palmistry tells us that an individual is an amalgam of many factors: genetic, environmental, and karmic. According to the theory of palmistry, all of these factors are recorded in the palms of the hands. At birth, both of our hands are very similar, and represent our genetic and karmic potentials. As we mature, our dominant hand—the hand we use most—changes to reflect the direction our life actually takes. Our passive hand changes much more slowly, thus retaining a record of the potential we brought into this life at birth. The dominant hand shows us which of these characteristics we've actually manifested. Not only does our passive hand show us what we could be, it shows us what we were meant to be.

My goal as a palmist is to try to ferret out useful information and find answers to life's more difficult questions. Nothing happens without a reason. What lessons do we learn from our disappointments and setbacks? Why do we strive so hard sometimes for so little reward?

We learn from Eastern thought that the challenges we face are caused by our personal karma, or the effects of our good and bad deeds from a previous life. From these struggles we learn certain lessons and gain information and skills that prepare us for the future. Sometimes these lessons are difficult, but along with our karma, we bring into this life the tools that help us deal with the difficulties. These tools can be found in the hand and—once recognized by the individual—encouraged to grow. In this way, palmistry can help us make our personal learning experiences less painful.

A curious fact is that the passive hand usually has many more lines than the dominant hand. This is because the passive hand begins where our previous life left off. It contains a concise record of the entire range of gifts, talents, dispositions, temperaments, and karma accumulated during our previous lifetime. The dominant hand shows us which of these traits and talents we've recognized, and how we've chosen to use them in our current existence.

Engraved on our hands at birth is the blueprint for the next stage of our spiritual development. If we, as parents, recognize this in our own children, we can follow this blueprint as the child matures. What a wonderful way to avoid the pitfalls of bad career choices, unfulfilling relationships, and unhappy lifestyles! We could continue our karmic work where we left it off, eventually achieve our potential, and become happy and productive people.

Unfortunately, life is rarely this simple. None of us is born into an ideal situation. We're under constant pressure to be something we're not. Parents, religious institutions, school, peers, childhood trauma—all of these pervasive influences affect the development of our personality and change us in ways that are not always compatible with our original character. We change, and not always for the better.

By adulthood, these changes are recorded on the dominant hand and can be clearly seen by comparing the two hands. This is why in palmistry the dominant hand is seen as the present time and the passive as the past. In over thirty years of reading hands, very rarely have I seen a person whose hands are identical.

Look at your own hands. Is the right hand significantly different from the left? Are the three major lines (life line, heart line, and head line; see Figure 0.1) the same on both hands, or do they differ? If they differ, then you will find this book especially useful. These differences reflect the ways our character changes as we react to the external pressures of life. Sometimes the differences in our hands reveal tests and temptations that must be confronted and conquered.

By comparing these simple differences we'll see how palmistry can help to diagnose an individual's karmic cycle, discover ways to maximize the quality of life, explore past lives, choose a satisfying career, find a soul mate, and assure a better existence for the future.

Of course, palmistry, like any psychic science, is not a clear window into the future. Some aspects of our karma are crystal clear, while others frustratingly elude our most determined efforts to understand them. Often, we seem to get information about every aspect of our lives except that which we want to know the most! Twenty years ago my house burned down and I lost all of my property. A friend of mine asked me a perfectly reasonable question: "How come you didn't see it coming?" At the time, I didn't know the answer to this; now I do. Just because a person is psychic doesn't exclude him or her from having to learn certain lessons. I was growing too attached to my possessions, and karma dictated that I needed a wake-up call. I needed to learn what was really important and permanent in life.

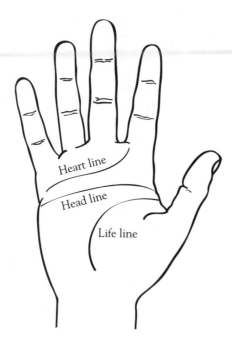

Heart line

Head line

Life line

Figure 0.1—The three major lines of the hand

Finally, I must insert a note about my previous book, *Runic Palmistry*. In that book, I presented a complete system of hand reading based on Norse mythology. In this book, rather than continue the Norse terminology, I've used nomenclature from classical palmistry so as not to confuse any readers who haven't read my previous work. I suggest, if you haven't already done so, that when you finish this book, go back and read *Runic Palmistry* for more techniques of hand reading.

I hope that I've been successful in sharing what I've learned about the connection between karma and hand reading. As you read this book, please remember that, as we're reminded by Zen masters, no written description of a glass of water will quench your thirst, nor will a picture of a fire, no matter how well executed, warm your bones in the winter. There's no substitute for experience, so try to apply these techniques to yourself and to those whom you love. I never cease to be amazed at how the beautiful diagnostic tools of palmistry can help us understand our own lives better, and by doing so, allow us to realize that the most wonderful gift any of us can give to the world is ourselves.

OLD SUFI STORY

A man approached the local mullah for advice. His neighbor, it seemed, was driving him crazy with his incessant, unannounced visits. How could he get him to stay away, or at least suggest he drop by less frequently, without offending him?

"Simple," said the mullah. "The next time he drops in, just ask if you can borrow some money. Continue to do this and before long he'll stop coming over."

The man was amazed. "But then my other neighbors will think I'm impoverished and can't fulfill my financial obligations," the man complained.

"Ah," said the mullah. "Now you want to change the thought patterns of everyone in the world. That's a different problem altogether!"

There is no cure for birth and death, save to enjoy the interval.

—George Santayana, *Skepticism and Animal Faith*

chapter one

PALMISTRY 101

The hand is the cutting edge of the mind.

—Jacob Bronowski, *The Ascent of Man*

*B*efore we plunge into the study of karmic palmistry, let's take a quick look at some of the fundamental principles of traditional palmistry.

Palmistry is the art of reading a person's character through the shape of the hands, the formation of the mounts of the hands, the fingers, and the lines that appear in the palm. Palmistry has enjoyed a fascinating history. It is believed to have been practiced in ancient India and China. Great heroes and spiritual leaders, such as the Buddha, have been recognized though palmistry.

The lines of the hand act as a sort of circuit board of the brain. Neurosurgeons tell us that these lines are caused by nerve endings in the palm. These nerves stem from the middle brain, where the two hemispheres join. Therefore, every thought you have, conscious and unconscious, is reflected in some way on your hand. As your life and attitudes change, the lines of your hand will reflect the new patterns of your life. This can be observed by studying your own hand closely. You may observe over time that your life line (the third of the three major lines; see also Figure 0.1) creeps across your palm as you experience dramatic changes in your life. The other lines of the hand change as well. It's important to remember that the lines change as your attitudes change, not vice versa. The tail does not wag the dog.

It's useful to have a set system from which to read; otherwise you'll get confused by the complexity of the first palm you come across and become discouraged. My system is simple and easy to remember. I start with the shape of the hand, analyze the length of the fingers, note any obvious mounts or valleys, and comment on the heart line, the head line, the life line, and the thumb. Then I move on to a more detailed analysis of spurs, islands, geometric shapes, and other complexities that are discussed later in this book. Actually, by working from the shape of the hand and the lines alone, you can give an excellent reading.

To obtain practice material, ask your friends to make photocopies or ink prints of their hands for you to study. Some of your acquaintances will think you're off your rocker, but you'll find just as many who are interested in what their hands tell you.

Collect several hand prints before you get started, and notice the amazing variety of different hand types. Some palmistry systems list as many as thirty different categories based on hand shapes alone. Then, start learning the shapes of the hand as discussed below. This alone will tell you a lot about the personality of the individual. Move on to finger length and mounts, then lastly, the lines. Don't try to learn everything at once; to become a good palm reader takes months or even years. I've been reading hands for over thirty years and I'm still learning.

I encourage you to work at developing your intuition. Your sensitivity and intuition contribute to the overall depth of the reading. You don't have to be psychic to read palms, but the intuitive ability gives you the insights and examples that bring life to your readings. You must give each reading the personal attention that will make the experience memorable, dramatic, and eclectic. A refined sense of intuition can help, and not only in doing readings, but also in relationships and with a career.

THE SHAPES

We'll be looking at the implications of hand shapes in much more detail in chapter 8, but for now we'll focus on four basic categories.

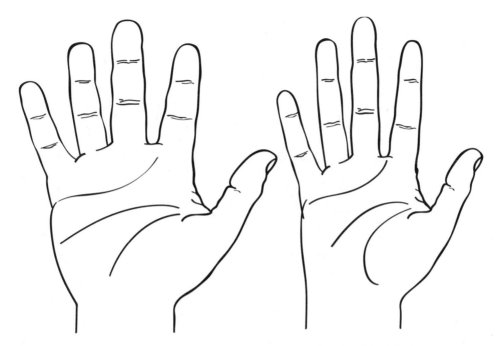

Figures 1.1 and 1.2—Earth hand (left) and air hand (right)

The Earth Hand

The earth hand is usually the easiest of the four types to recognize. The qualities to look for are a square, fleshy palm, short fingers, and very few lines (Figure 1.1). The few lines reflect a preference for simplicity. If the fingers are rounded at the tips, the person may be a bit impatient. Square tips suggest a person who thinks a little bit more before he or she acts.

The subject possessing an earth hand will be practical, reliable, predictable, emotionally stable, and often conservative. The line patterns of these hands are usually very simple, which reflects the person's simple and direct approach to life.

The Air Hand

Recognizable by its square palm and long fingers, the air hand denotes a person with a quick, agile mind (Figure 1.2). The negative side of air types is their tendency to

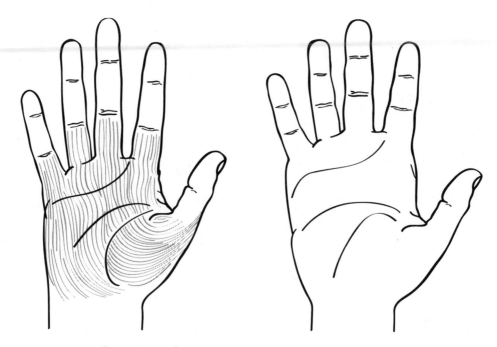

Figures 1.3 and 1.4—Water hand (left) and fire hand (right)

deceive and manipulate. Air types are great self-motivators and work according to their own inner agenda. They can be a bit flamboyant in their behavior, sometimes acting in a contrived manner to elicit a desired response from others. Consequently, they don't always mean what they say.

The Water Hand

A water hand has a rectangular palm, is very soft and flexible, and has many fine lines and long, smoothly tapered fingers (Figure 1.3). Water types tend to be moody, and at times their external appearance is completely at odds with the internal reality. "You can't judge a book by its cover" is definitely true of a water type. They can be difficult to please. The long fingers denote perfectionism and sensitivity to detail. Because of the myriad tiny lines covering the surface, water hands tend to look old. However, the lines have nothing to do with age. Instead, they indicate the intensity of this type's emotional expression.

The Fire Hand

Fire hands have short fingers, which denote impatience, with a long palm, which indicates their vast reserves of emotional energy (Figure 1.4). The fire hand is usually hot to the touch. People with this hand type are passionate and intense. They love change and variety, and become easily bored with tedious work. They hate restrictions, limitations, or falling into a rut.

THE FINGERS

The length and shape of the fingers can reveal a lot about a person's emotional expression. Basically—and very generally—people with long fingers tend to be open-minded and flexible, but can be a bit perfectionistic. People with short fingers can be very stubborn and impatient. They want answers right now, and they like very specific answers to specific questions.

Length of Individual Fingers

The relative length of each individual finger can tell about the person's emotional quirks.

- A long forefinger (the finger of Jupiter) denotes an aggressive, bossy person.

- A long second finger (the finger of Saturn) represents someone whose conscience is very strong.

- A long ring finger (the finger of Apollo) represents someone who is an idealist, but who has the ability to motivate others through his or her strong personal magnetism.

- A long little finger (the finger of Mercury) denotes someone with a natural fluency with words—a born salesperson. An extremely long Mercury denotes someone who bends the truth to suit him- or herself, so this person may not always necessarily mean what he or she says.

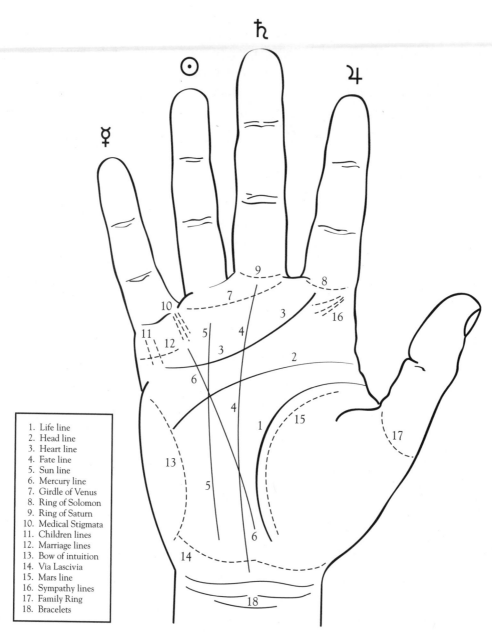

1. Life line
2. Head line
3. Heart line
4. Fate line
5. Sun line
6. Mercury line
7. Girdle of Venus
8. Ring of Solomon
9. Ring of Saturn
10. Medical Stigmata
11. Children lines
12. Marriage lines
13. Bow of intuition
14. Via Lascivia
15. Mars line
16. Sympathy lines
17. Family Ring
18. Bracelets

Figure 1.5—The lines of the hand

THE LINES

At last! The lines of the hand are what give palmists the most material for interpretation and analysis. The interpretation of the palm lines is called *chiromancy*. First, familiarize yourself with Figure 1.5.

There are three major lines to start with, but as you can see from the figure, there are many more lines you can use to fine-tune your reading. The three major lines are described below.

The Life Line (1)

The life line is the line that wraps around the thumb and ends at the wrist. Contrary to legend, the length of the life line cannot be used to predict the life span of the individual. This is inaccurate and can do absolutely no good. However, the life line gives us a good idea of the person's life energies, and how directed the person is. As you read a lot of palms, you'll learn to distinguish the various energy levels between the two extremes.

- A shallow life line means that the life energies are weak, and the person tends to be tired a lot. He or she may tend to procrastinate and put off unpleasant necessities.

- A strong life line means that the person is vital and energetic; his or her energies are high and very focused. The person is very directed and goal-oriented.

- A life line that hugs in close to the thumb denotes a homebody; home and hearth will mean a great deal to this person.

- A line that sweeps out across the hand denotes someone with an "itchy foot"; this person will travel a lot because he or she tends to be restless. Once again, there are many shades of gray in this area; you'll find very few "pure" palms.

- Spurs and lines shooting off from the life line can indicate up and down periods in the person's life. Spurs that shoot toward the wrist indicate down periods, while upward spurs indicate happy periods.

The Head Line (2)

The head line is the line that starts at the side of the hand, just above the life line, and travels horizontally across the palm. The head line denotes patterns of thought and tells us if a person is logical or imaginative in his or her approach to problem solving. Where the head line ends is of the utmost significance.

- A head line that is straight and points to the heel of the hand belongs to a practical, logical person. This person prefers a direct approach to life and tends to see things in terms of black and white. He or she can be somewhat of a perfectionist.

- A head line that curves in toward the wrist denotes a person who is imaginative and creative in his or her approach to life and problem-solving.

  The curvier the line, the more imaginative the approach. If the line travels far down into the heel of the hand, you have someone who's a bit of a dreamer, and who will have to focus on making his or her ambitions realistic.

The Heart Line (3)

The heart line is a very interesting line, because most people want to know about their romantic prospects. You could make a good living simply by reading the heart line alone. Since I don't believe that palmistry can pinpoint future events—at least not without taking into account the effects of karma—you can't predict the exact date when someone will meet the person of his or her dreams by studying the heart line alone. However, if you can get a feel for how the person thinks and for some of his or her emotional strategies, and you know a lot about human behavior patterns, you can make a few good, shrewd guesses about the person's future. A little intuition and clairvoyant ability helps too.

The heart line starts at the edge of the hand above the head line, and travels across the hand toward the thumb side. Where the heart line ends is important.

- If the heart line ends under the first finger, it denotes a strong romantic who may put partners on a pedestal. This person may be the type who falls in love with love.

- A heart line that ends under the second finger denotes someone who is flamboyant and dynamic in his or her affections. Watch out! You may get your head hugged off. People with this line love to show their affection and receive great satisfaction from helping others.

- A heart line that travels up into the second finger is very rare and known as the *Gift of Mercy*. These people are capable of great, loving sacrifice in the service of others. Mother Teresa had this formation.

- When the heart line ends between the first and second fingers, there's a good, balanced approach to love. The person is able to give and receive affection appropriately, and won't get caught up in another and lose sight of him- or herself. This also indicates a healthy enjoyment of physical love.

Very few people have a perfectly balanced heart line. You'll notice little forks, islands, and spurs shooting off of it, which denote hard lessons learned in the school of love. Sometimes you will notice two heart lines. This is known as the *Girdle of Venus* (7), which can indicate extreme sensitivity, or as some believe, circulatory problems.

Other Lines

Look at Figure 1.5 to locate the following lines.

- The fate line (4) travels vertically up the palm and denotes the person's ambitions. Traditionally, a long, straight fate line indicates someone with good drive and focus. A splintered, forked, or interrupted line denotes uncertainty on the life path. The person could be at odds with him- or herself.

- The Sun line (5) is a good line to have, as it signifies success in worldly endeavors. It can indicate fame, popularity, and attachment to an expensive lifestyle.

- The Mercury line (6) is a mark of amazing communication skills. People with this line are natural salespeople, very chatty and charming, and communicate well with others.

- The Girdle of Venus (7) has already been discussed in connection with the heart line. It indicates extreme emotional sensitivity and empathy.

- The Ring of Solomon (8) denotes psychic ability and wisdom.

- The Ring of Saturn (9) shows an old soul; someone who is wise beyond his or her years. It can indicate a natural teacher or spiritual leader.

- The Medical Stigmata (10) is a sign of a natural healer.

- As we'll see in chapter 6, children lines (11) do not necessarily show the number of children you will have, but the number of children you are capable of parenting. Often people express this parenting need though pets, other people's children, or by working with kids in their spare time.

- As we'll see in chapter 6, marriage lines (12) are like children lines in that they do not necessarily show how many marriages you will have, but the number of soul mates you will encounter during your life.

- The Bow of Intuition (13) is self-explanatory. This indicates a naturally strong sense of intuition.

- The Via Lascivia (14) gives the owner an above-average interest in sex.

- The Mars line (15) represents increased success, assertiveness, and competitive skills. Some schools of palmistry associate this sign with the presence of a protective spirit (see chapter 6).

- Sympathy lines (16) give a person a sympathetic, understanding outlook.

- The Family Ring (17) shows that the person has a great love for home and hearth, and that family will always be important.

- Bracelets or rascettes (18) act as extra life lines and add strength, alertness, and virility to the person as he or she advances in years.

PUTTING IT ALL TOGETHER

It's rarely necessary or desirable in a quick reading to tell a person everything you see. Long, detailed readings can become blurred in the individual's recollection. There's a lot to be said for the short-and-sweet approach.

If you do other sorts of psychic readings, such as Tarot cards or runestones, you can use quick palm readings to add variety. A palm reading for entertainment (such as you might deliver at a party, for example) shouldn't go over ten minutes.

Also, it's important to be positive. People tend to take readings very seriously, and often will act on what you say. Remember, we're not qualified to offer medical, legal, or financial advice. Try to always end on an upbeat note. Good luck!

Oh, who can read the stars like the Egyptians [Gypsies]? And who can read the palm like them?

—George Barrow, *The Zincal*

chapter two
THE LAW OF KARMA

Peter said to him [Jesus], "Since you have explained everything to us, tell us this also: What is the sin of the world?"

The Savior said, "There is no sin, but it is you who make sin."

—*The Gnostic Gospel of Mary Magdalene*
(The Akhmim Codex)

*K*arma is a topic that has been the subject of thousands of books and centuries of thought. The concept is pivotal to every Eastern religion, and more than a few Western philosophies. The concept of karma is universal; all cultures recognize it in one form or another. It has inspired such homilies as "You reap what you sow," "What goes around comes around," and the motto of the 1930s radio crime fighter the Shadow, "The weed of crime bears bitter fruit."

Depending on the culture, the concept of karma has several different interpretations. While some schools of thought use the term to mean a sort of payback for our good and bad deeds, others (notably Buddhist scholars) maintain that karma never means the *effect* of a good or a bad deed, but the deed itself. This initial deed, they argue, sets into motion a chain of events that leads to either good or bad situations, depending on the nature of the original deed. Edgar Cayce, on the other hand, taught that the consequences of our actions in this life were not karma, but simply cause and effect. He said that karma was always what we bring into this life as consequences from a past life.

In spite of these differing approaches to the precise mechanism of karma, one thing is perfectly clear. Everyone agrees that karma is connected to action. The word *karma* is derived from the Sanskrit term *kr*, which means "action" or "deed." Therefore, any deliberate action—physical or mental—is the essential motivating force of the karmic process. For our purposes, we will use the term in its most general sense to describe the entire karmic process:

$$\text{Action} \longrightarrow \text{Effect} \longrightarrow \text{Reaction} \longrightarrow \text{Effect} \longrightarrow \text{etc.}$$

There is a cause (action) and an effect (result)—both are karma. Furthermore, we react to the result of the initial deed, and this produces more effects, and so on, forever and ever, like ever-widening ripples on a pond; all of this is karma.

We mustn't underestimate the effects of karma on our body, mind, and spirit. Karma is the reason we are born into this world in the first place, and why we are reborn again and again through numberless lifetimes. Karma determines the time and place of our birth, and whether we are born into affluent circumstances or miserable poverty. Karma is the source of all of our challenges and the armory from which we draw the necessary weapons to face them. Karma truly makes the world go 'round—at least as far as people are concerned.

THE KARMIC CYCLE

The karmic cycle begins with a conscious decision to perform an action. Actions in a karmic sense are not only physical deeds, but also words, thoughts, and attitudes. The unskillful physical actions of karma include:

- Killing

- Stealing

- Sexual misconduct

- Acts of malicious speech

- Lying

- Troublemaking

- Harsh words and gossip

Some of the unskillful mental actions of karma are:

- Greed

- Envy

- Wishing harm to come to others

- Hate

- Self-delusion

- Ignorance

Skillful actions, of course, are:

- Compassion

- Generosity

- Humility

- Positive attitude

- Kindness

- Honesty

We decide whether our actions are skillful or unskillful, and we alone are responsible for the results these decisions set into motion.

Although we are in the habit of categorizing things as good and bad, in a karmic sense there are no good or evil actions. As you've seen above, actions are either skillful or unskillful. Negative, or unskilled, actions produce chaos and conflict, and torture our minds with anxiety, remorse, worry, and fear. Unskillful actions may also attract bad luck and misfortune, and, in extreme cases, death, personal injury, or severe emotional illness. Furthermore, our careless actions can cause harm to others and generate conflict in the world around us. This web of conflict—the result of negative actions in this lifetime or those previous—is commonly called "bad karma"; although, as pointed out earlier, there's really no such thing as good or bad when discussing karmic issues.

Not only does karma explain all the unpleasant things that happen to us, it is also responsible for the good things: friends, loved ones, good experiences, happiness, and joy. All of these positive experiences are in our lives as a direct result of past karma.

Karma is not a vague metaphysical theory, but the cause-and-effect nature of reality. If we drop a hammer on our toes (cause), the action will produce pain and injury (effect). If we tickle a baby under his or her chin (cause), the baby will reward us with delighted giggles that produce good feelings (effect). In either case, the physical action was preceded by a mental action—the decision to act—which set into motion the law of karma.

For example, when a person commits a crime, the consequences of the wrongdoing will be severe whether or not legal punishment follows. A criminal suffers far more than legal punishment or fear of discovery alone could cause. His or her personality is affected by the guilt, remorse, and stress generated by the commission of the crime. The victims may demand restitution or punishment. Also, the commission of crimes may lead to a coarsening of personality that will make it more likely for the person to commit similar crimes in the future. We can easily see how unskillful action not only harms others, but also damages the body, mind, and spirit of the person responsible.

It doesn't end there; the results of that initial hostile action will produce results of their own, and those results will produce even more. Thus we see that negative acts perpetuate an environment that becomes increasingly dangerous and unpleasant. Multiply this process by every living being in the universe and we begin to see the vast power karma has in shaping the very world in which we live.

Of course, karma is a two-way street. It requires both an action and a reaction. Suppose someone speaks harshly to you. If you respond harshly, you, too, are generating negative karma by perpetuating the cycle of negativity. The other person is likely to react to your response with further anger, and the cycle will continue, blow for blow. However (and this is a beautiful thing), if you respond to the initial negative act skillfully—with kindness, compassion, and forgiveness—the bad results of karma can go no further. In addition, you have discharged some of your own karmic debt (discussed in detail in chapter 4) in direct proportion to the negative karma you avoided. Not only does a soft answer "turneth away wrath," it also breaks the cycle of negative karma. This is important, for the karma we accumulate follows us through all of our reincarnations, forever and ever.

"GOOD KARMA"

As mentioned earlier, not all karma is negative. The fruits of positive or skillful thoughts, words, and deeds are collectively known as "merit" or "good karma." Merit, like the fruit of bad karma, has long-term effects. Merit is also cumulative. Once accrued, it can be used to improve the quality of our present circumstances, and ensure our rebirth into a relatively pleasant future existence. Merit gives one peace of mind, serenity, and happiness. Most importantly, merit reduces the amount of karmic debt we accumulate, helps loosen the bonds of the world, and speeds our release from the cycle of birth, death, and rebirth.

Our karma can be changed through positive action. The Chinese Buddhist physiognomists (face and hand readers) relate a story from the ancient book of divination called Ma-i, which was written about a thousand years ago. The story illustrates how personal action can alter karma.

It seems there was once an old man who was well versed in face and hand reading, and he had a young servant. One day, the old man noticed certain signs in his young servant's face and hands that indicated the poor boy had less than a month to live. Being a compassionate man, the old master didn't mention the boy's fate to him. Instead, he sent the servant home for a "vacation," so that the servant would die with his family. The boy, never suspecting that his days were numbered, packed his belongings and set upon the journey to his village.

About a month later the old man heard a noise in the front room of his house. When he investigated it, imagine his amazement at seeing his young servant returning from his "vacation" in perfect health! Being wise, the old man knew there had to be more to the story than met the eye. The master asked the boy to tell him every-thing that happened since the boy left the master's home.

The boy told him that on his way home, he saw a colony of ants on a piece of wood in a stream. He realized that when the water rose, the ants would drown. So, having learned compassion from his master, he constructed a bridge from wood and stone so the ants could travel safely to shore. The old man nodded with understanding. "Karma decreed that you were meant to die, but your act of com-passion earned you the gift of life." The old master realized that nothing was irrevocably decreed by fate, and that good deeds can change the course of any-one's future.

Karma, as this story points out, is not inflexible, but subject to change accord-ing to our actions.

We don't have to devote our lives to studying Zen to assure a pleasant future. All we have to do is act the way we know we should. Any time we help another living being, we help ourselves, and if we deliberately hurt another living being, it comes back to haunt us. This concept isn't exclusive to Buddhists, it's a recurring theme in most world religions. It is clear that Jesus Christ understood this natural law when he taught, "Do unto others as you would have them do unto you."

Understanding karma and its effects helps us make sense of our lives. As we explore our personal karma, we begin to realize that nothing—absolutely noth-ing—happens without a reason. Our fate is not determined by random chance, nor is it meted out by a higher power. Karma isn't punishment for sin, as is some-times popularly believed, nor is it reward for good behavior. There is no cosmic authority sitting in judgment of our actions. It is not a higher power that punishes us for our misdeeds or rewards us for acts of charity; we reap what we sow by our own deliberate actions. Skillful actions produce good results; unskillful actions produce bad results.

Karma is cause and effect; personal, immediate, and completely under our control. So when we ask the question, "Why is life so hard?" the answer is "Because you've made it so." When we ask, "What did I do to deserve such good luck, terrific health, and such wonderful friends?", the answer is the same.

KARMA VS. FATE

The Western concept of predetermination can lead one to the conclusion that we're all helpless prisoners of fate, doomed to play out a script written for us at birth. This is not the case at all with the Eastern concept of karma. Through the study of Buddhism and Chinese divination systems such as the I Ching, we learn that our karma shows us a Way, and that it is possible to follow this Way to a better life. Our decisions and our actions determine the course of our present existence and our future lives. Karma and free will work together—the yin and yang of our destiny. Karma provides us with the potential to learn lessons we need in order for our soul to grow. Free will, on the other hand, determines whether or not we choose to learn the lessons at this time or put them off for a future time.

With free will, we can either turn our challenges into stepping stones toward growth, or we can see them as obstacles and stumbling blocks. Either way, we'll reap what we sow. It's almost a cliché that if we refuse to learn from a negative experience, we're doomed to repeat it. Certain events in our lives must be experienced and certain lessons learned in order for us to grow into the person we were meant to be. The choices we make now determine the next set of potential experiences we'll encounter in the future.

That brings us to the purpose of this book: learning about ourselves and our karma through the study of the hands. In the next chapter we will have a short discussion about reincarnation and how karma influences the circumstances of our birth. Don't go away!

> *There is no end*
> *There is no beginning.*
> *There is only the infinite passion of life.*
>
> —Frederico Fellini, *Fellini on Fellini*

chapter three

REINCARNATION
& THE KARMIC CYCLE

I sent my Soul through the Invisible
Some letter of the life after to spell
Soon my Soul returned to me
And said "I myself am both Heaven and
*   Hell."*

—Omar Khayyam, *The Rubiyat*

Reincarnation is the belief that when we die we are reborn as other people. In other words, our souls move into a new body as the old body passes away. The concept of the rebirth of the soul appears in the three major Eastern religions: Buddhism, Hinduism, and Jainism. Among the ancient Greeks, reincarnation was associated with the followers of philosopher and mathematician Pythagoras. Among Jews, the mystical believers in the Kabala adopted it as part of their philosophical system. Among Christians, the Gnostics and the Manichaeans believed in reincarnation, but the church condemned those who adopted the doctrine as heretics. In the Bagavad Gita, an ancient Hindu spiritual text, we are told, "The disembodied soul clothes itself in new bodies as we don a new cloak."

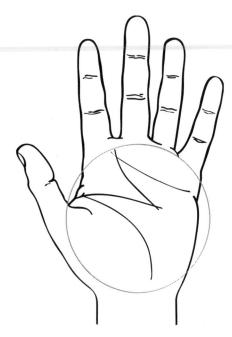

Figure 3.1—A sign of an old soul

Some people have been reincarnated very few times. Others have been reincarnated countless times and are known as "old souls" due not to their age in chronological years, but to the wisdom they have learned throughout the centuries. Old souls can be spotted by several signs in the hand, such as a large letter M composed of the head line, heart line, fate line, and life line (Figure 3.1). A Ring of Saturn, discussed in chapter 1, can denote an old soul. Also, a large number of very deeply graven creases indicate an old soul, as though each successive life etches itself more firmly in his or her hand.

Another traditional sign of an old soul is known as an *Old Soul's Mount* (Figure 3.2). A very rare trait, this is an exaggerated Mount of Pluto that lies well down on the wrist. When you find one of these, you know you're looking at the sign of a very advanced soul.

You don't have to be an expert palmist to spot an old soul. Old souls can be spotted at birth by looking into their eyes. They are calm and have a mature air about them, even when only a few minutes old.

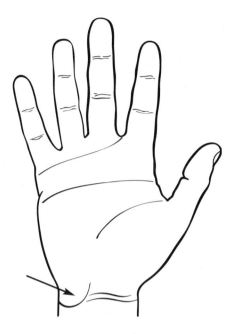

Figure 3.2—"Old Soul's Mount"

DO WE COME BACK AS ANIMALS?

The belief that humans can be reincarnated as animals is called *transmigration*. Buddha spoke of several of his past lives as animals, including one in particular where he was an elephant who, while dying at the hands of a hunter, helped the man remove his own tusks. Many religions teach that human souls can be reincarnated as animals, and vice versa. (My father-in-law says he wants to come back as one of my mother-in-law's cats!) The idea is that souls evolve from the simplest life forms to the more complex, climbing the karmic ladder with each incarnation. Furthermore, if our actions are exceptionally unskillful, we may have to return to a lower state after we die and become reborn as an animal or insect.

Many people wrongly believe that animals do not have souls or sensibilities, and act only on instinct. Anyone who has ever formed a close emotional bond with a pet knows this simply isn't true. Not only are pets members of our earthly families, but often they are members of our soul families as well, and reincarnate along with the rest of us. I've had cats all my life, and I firmly believe that I have had the same cat three different times.

I must confess that I'm undecided on the issue. In my own experience, people seem to always come back as people and animals as animals. Wild animals appear to have their own karmic lessons and karmic laws, which seem unrelated to those of human spirits. Domesticated animals, however, do seem to have a spiritual and karmic agenda to work in concert with humans toward the betterment of both the human and the animal.

Then again, would we remember a past life as, say, a grasshopper? If so, what would we remember? Does that recurring dream about being eaten by a giant bird have more significance than we thought?

While this chapter will only deal with the dynamics of what happens when we return as humans, I do want to share with you a story about my first exposure to the concept of karmic rebirth. This story illustrates the darker side of the trans-migration question—the idea that if our deeds are unskillful enough, our souls will retrograde into a lower form until we accumulate enough merit to come back again as human beings.

As you may know if you've read my previous book, *Runic Palmistry*, I learned a great deal of my craft from my grandmother and her sister, Great-Aunt Eliza. Both my grandmother and Aunt Eliza believed in reincarnation. Oddly enough, a lot of rural and mountain people of the southeast U.S. believe in reincarnation in some form or other.

In the summer of 1972, I was about twelve years old. My family and I were vis-iting Aunt Eliza and her husband, Uncle Vondous, on their little farm in Bull's Gap, Tennessee. We didn't know it at the time, but Vondous had a time bomb ticking away in his head that would explode into a sudden, fatal stroke in less than a year. At the moment however, he was sitting on the porch with my dad swapping laughter and drinks from a brown bottle.

The momentum of the sixties was still sweeping through the country, bringing with it an interest in Eastern philosophies. My brother and I had received a boxed gift set of the I Ching the previous Christmas, and we struggled through it for hours, trying to figure out what flying dragons and lotus blossoms had to do with whether or not we'd pass our exams!

I had been reading a bit about reincarnation and had quite a few questions about the process, especially the concept of karma. Naturally, I sought the advice of the family know-it-all, Aunt Eliza. She was more than willing to talk at length about the subject.

During our conversation I asked Aunt Eliza about people who caused a great deal of suffering during their life, like Adolf Hitler. It didn't seem to me that he paid adequately for his actions. People were always saying, "What goes around comes around," but what price did he pay? Oh sure, he had to commit suicide, I said, but he was responsible for the deaths of millions. How come he didn't have to pay? Why didn't something horrible happen to him?

Aunt Eliza looked stern. "Who are you to say whether Hitler paid or not? Are you privy to his private thoughts? Do you have any way of knowing what kind of spiritual suffering he may have gone through before his death?"

No, I admitted, but dying once didn't seem like a fair trade for the slaughter of millions.

Aunt Eliza nodded. "Nor does it to me, either. He was a son of a bitch for sure. But as I say, we don't know everything."

I guess I had to be content with that. Changing the subject, I asked her if she believed we came back in nonhuman forms, such as animals or insects.

Aunt Eliza replied, "I think we do. A soul is a soul, it doesn't have a body. It depends on how we behave in this life whether or not we come back as people, or as something else."

I told her that, judging from the carefree life of the animals on the farm, it seemed easier on us if we came back as animals, or even as a bug; no school, no chickenpox, all your food for free.

She smiled. "You think so, Jonny? You really think so?" Seeing that smile, I knew I was in for a wake-up call. "Let's go for a walk. I want to show you something."

We walked across the backyard and through the rose arbor. The speckled shade was a welcome relief from the blistering heat of midafternoon. We emerged on the other side of the cool arbor back into the full blast of the summer sun.

Aunt Eliza stopped and pointed to a small lump on the hot, paved driveway. "Looky here," she said.

I knelt down and saw that the lump was a dead baby bird that had fallen from its nest and died on the hot pavement. The sight of the pitiful thing hurt my heart. "This is nature, Jonny," she said. "Some live, some die. Some die bad. That little feller fell from his nest and died of hunger and thirst on this hot pavement, all alone. What did he do to deserve it, while his brothers and sisters ate their fill of fat worms just a few feet away?"

I shook my head. I had no answer. We kept walking until we came to the small pear and apple orchard where Aunt Eliza harvested the makings of her spectacular cobblers. She showed me a spider web. "Look at the spider," she said. "Look closely."

I did; the spider had an ugly growth on it that was almost as big as its body. "What's wrong with his back?" I asked.

Aunt Eliza pointed into the woods. "There's a nest of wasps back there," she said, "that paralyze its prey—like that little spider—lay its eggs into the bug's body, and let it go on its way. The bug lives its life normally, like this spider has—spinning its web, and eating flies and daddy long-legs. Until one day the wasp's eggs hatch inside its body and the baby wasps eat the spider alive from the inside out." She pointed to the little spider. "That little feller has only a few days to go before he's in for a big surprise."

I looked at her in shock and distress. After all, I was twelve years old—raised with Disney movies and a year away from reading *The Origin of Species*—and this lesson in the relentless ways of nature was a bit unsettling. Eliza sat on a rock and looked at me solemnly, and I'll never forget what she said that day. "You asked me earlier today about Hitler. Now mind you, it's not my place to say I understand the will of God. But if I were God, maybe, just maybe, Hitler would come back as that baby bird, dying helplessly in the sun. And as that spider, eaten alive by another bug's children and not understanding why. And I would make him do it again and again, until his debt was paid, one life for every one he took. Hell, I'd settle for one in ten."

She stood up and stretched. "But I suspect I'm a little bit meaner than God, and a lot less patient with human error. Just remember to be a good boy and you won't have to worry about coming back as someone else's dinner." She smiled at me. "Believe me, coming back as people is far better, and that's all you need to know about reincarnation."

This was my first exposure to the idea that reincarnation was nature's way of evening the score. Whether you believe in the points made by my old aunt or not, you have to admit it was an unforgettable lesson. Later that afternoon, I watched my uncle and my grandfather castrate a pig. To this day I try my damnedest to be a good boy!

THE KARMIC CYCLE OF BIRTH AND REBIRTH

The mechanism of reincarnation is simple. When we die, all of our personality traits die with us, but the desire for sensual experience (to think, act, talk; to achieve wealth and status; to learn lessons that can only be learned while in a physical body) sets into motion a series of events that lead to our soul's rebirth as another, different person. This new person comes into existence as a result of the karma created by this desire, and therefore inherits all the accumulated karma of his or her previous lifetime, both positive and negative.

When we're ready, our soul enters the developing embryo within our mother's womb, and begins the process of preparing the physical body for rebirth into the world. We're helped in this task by spiritual beings whose role is to assist us in preparing for the challenges we intend to face. These beings (members of our karmic family; chapter 6) help us create our "blueprint"—the lessons, gifts, and karmic challenges we plan on facing in the new life.

This karmic blueprint begins to become etched into our hands by the eighteenth week of pregnancy in the form of the three major lines: head, heart, and life. This fact alone disproves the skeptics' opinion that the creases of the hands are caused by flexure alone. We have hand lines long before the fingers are developed enough to flex! In fact, according to charts found in embryological texts such as *The Stages of Human Development before Birth* by E. Blechsmidt, the life line forms first, the heart line next, and the head line last, proving that first we live, then we feel, then we think.

During this time, we carefully pick and choose the talents and gifts we're going to need to confront the challenges of our new existence. A major part of our blueprint is karma carried over from previous lives.

Edgar Cayce, the great clairvoyant, taught that there are certain fundamental spiritual lessons such as love, moderation, balance, patience, and faith, which we attempt to learn during our souls' physical incarnations. However, there is conflict between our soul and our physical body, which stands in our way. On the one hand, our souls are one with everything and want for nothing—the soul is perfect, complete, and free from desire. However, as humans distracted by the needs of the flesh, we want for many things. We dimly sense that we lack something essential, and that obtaining more of this mysterious something will make us happy. Some of us want to be rich and famous; others may want to find the perfect mate who will fulfill everything we lack—our "soul mate." What we forget is that all these things we desire—material items, romantic love, success—are in reality useless to our soul, which already possesses all the strengths and abilities we'll ever need. Our task as human beings is to learn to use our abilities wisely. When we neglect this task we accumulate negative karma, which leads to karmic debt.

KARMIC DEBT

Negative karma that is carried over from another lifetime is called *karmic debt*. Karmic debt builds not only when we do wrong, but also whenever we fail to do what we know we should. Sins of omission are as great as sins of commission. The Japanese have a word for the work a person does simply because it needs doing: *tashinamu*. The person does the work without expecting reward or praise, and not even admitting to it giving a sense of satisfaction or pride. The idea is to do it and not let anyone know about it.

Ridding ourselves of karmic debt and accumulating merit is extremely important. We're motivated to do this not only to assure a better future life for ourselves, but also to satisfy our moral obligation to encourage an environment that promotes happiness and freedom for others.

How is karmic debt paid? Usually through difficult circumstances and trials. Once again, this is not punishment for our past misdeeds. It's simply debt, and all debts must be resolved. Payment can take many forms. For example, one of the consequences of negative karma is a tendency to be subjected to what our previous victim experienced; we ourselves may become the victim of similar acts committed by others. If we misused power in our past life, we will have to learn to restrain our arrogance in this lifetime. If we acted selfishly and miserly in a previous existence, we must learn generosity.

Karmic debt explains the mystery of why bad things often happen to good people. Sometimes we're tempted to say, "I don't know why so many bad things happen to me . . . I'm such a good person!" The answer is that we're paying the karmic debt from negative actions committed in our previous lives. This sometimes seems unfair, but karma is neither fair nor unfair; it simply is. Bear in mind that we also enjoy the benefits of past merit in the form of all the good things in our life. So when something wonderful, amazing, and blessed happens in our lives, when we're tempted to ask what we ever did to deserve such loving friends, lucky breaks, or spiritual joys, just remember that the answer is always the same: karma! Even while we're whittling away at our karmic debt, we're allowed to enjoy the benefits of our positive actions.

We all have a debt to pay, otherwise we wouldn't be here. In order to pay this debt, when confronted with misfortune or adversity, we must face the situation bravely and with understanding, and learn whatever skills are necessary to deal with the challenge. Knowledge is power, and karma causes us to place ourselves in situations from which we gain the knowledge necessary to discharge our debt. Hence, these situations are called *karmic lessons*.

DETERMINING KARMIC DEBT

We've already learned that the passive hand reveals the karma we bring into this life at birth. To determine the amount of karmic debt we have, we look at the heel of the passive hand (Figures 3.3 and 3.3A).

Most of us have a number of lines that stretch along the Mount of Venus and toward the life line. In classical palmistry these are called *worry lines* (or sometimes, *interference lines*). Since the passive hand represents the person we are at the moment of birth, these worries and stresses can only have been carried over from our previous life. Therefore, worry lines on the passive hand represent karmic debts, or lessons we must learn during our lifetime.

Now, examine the same area of your dominant hand. Are there more or less worry lines? If you find more, you decided to take on a great many karmic lessons in this lifetime. In other words, you really accelerated your learning curve! Your life was probably difficult, but will get easier in the future if you work through your lessons diligently. If there are fewer lines, you've learned a great many karmic

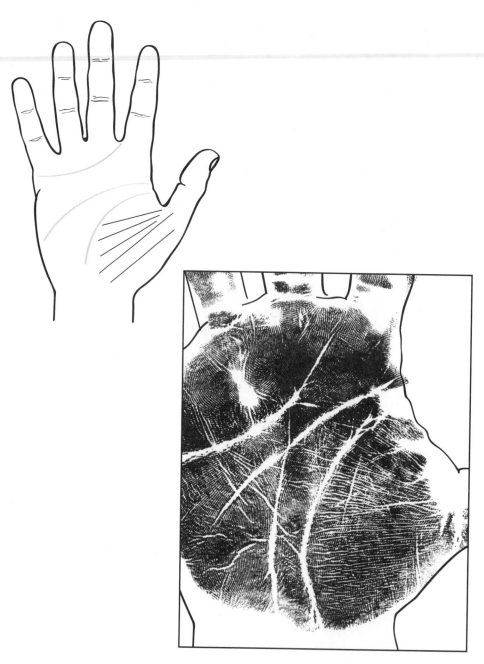

Figures 3.3 and 3.3A—Worry lines

lessons and have accumulated a good amount of merit. If the area is completely clear, congratulations—you can look forward to a blessed future incarnation!

KARMA AND STRESS

We recognize karmic lessons from the situations that subject us to stress. How stress affects us, the experts say, has little to do with the source of the stress but everything to do with how we react to it. The location of the worry lines can help us pinpoint the sources of our stressful karmic lessons, and give us useful hints on how to deal with them.

The shaded area of Figure 3.4 shows the area of family aggravation. This represents worry and stress caused by other people. When I mention to people that they have a lot of congestion in this area, they usually give a rueful laugh. If you were born into a difficult family, this area would have many lines! However, it was our decision before birth to be born into a difficult family situation in order to learn certain lessons, such as patience, understanding, and compassion. The challenge presented here is to learn to distance yourself from the family melodrama and be an observer. Remember that all the arguments, conflicts, and strife are your family's karma, not yours. How you react to the drama, however, is your karma. Family is family, and we have to love them no matter what.

Another cause of stress in this area is an overprotective attitude toward other people, especially loved ones and children. This usually indicates a reaction to losses incurred in the previous life. To counter this fear, we must learn to relax control and realize that nothing in this life is permanent or unchanging. Change is part of life, and attempting to resist change only produces more conflict. People with these lines must learn to loosen the paternal hold on their children and other loved ones. Often, the person is addicted to control and must learn to delegate responsibility to others. This sometimes requires serious work on trust issues.

The source of this hypervigilance seems to be rooted in the person's intuitive awareness of his or her karmic debt. People like this often feel that they owe it to the world to be super-responsible. Nobody could ever accomplish the tasks they set for themselves. To lower stress, they must lower the demands they make of themselves. I often say to them, "You don't always have to be the responsible one, you know." I also ask them what they think they're paying for by being so protective of

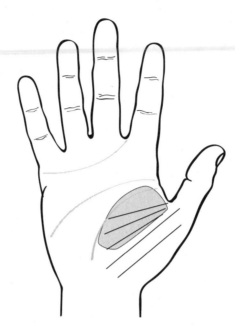

Figure 3.4—Area of family aggravation

everyone. Quite often, when we explore their past lives, we'll find a situation where the person's irresponsible behavior led to some negative consequence. Even though they don't consciously remember this episode, they're damned determined that it will never happen again. Once the cause of the fear is understood, the fear itself usually evaporates.

As we move down the pad of the thumb halfway between the life line and the wrist (Figure 3.5), we journey deeper and deeper into the subconscious mind. Worry lines in this area represent mental anxieties, fears, and phobias.

Those with a lot of congestion in this area are usually extremely sensitive about what other people think of them. They try very hard to meet other people's expectations. The person also worries about the future, which produces a great deal of fear.

Jiddhu Krishnamurti, an influential thinker from the Theosophical Buddhist tradition, points out that fear is always projected in time. We're never afraid of the present moment. We're afraid that something might happen in the future, or that

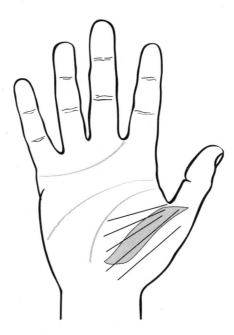

Figure 3.5—Worry lines in the area of mental anxieties

something that happened to us in the past might happen again. These are fears of the imagination and they rarely come true. Furthermore, these worries and anxieties often prevent us from enjoying the blessings of the current moment. Living in the present moment—the only one in which we can truly act—has a stabilizing effect. "We are here, and it is now," H. L. Mencken observed. "Further than that, all human knowledge is moonshine."

Zen Buddhists work toward eliminating suffering and anxiety through total concentration on the present moment. Past and future events have no power if one is totally focused on the now. Interestingly enough, this principle of "nowness" was independently preached by the German Dominican mystic Meister Johannes Eckhart, who lived between the eleventh and twelfth centuries B.C.E. Before his sermons were declared heretical, Meister Eckhart preached the sacredness of living in the current moment to hundreds of students. Eckhart taught that the unbroken unity of the universe existed in an eternal Now, and that the soul is troubled by the illusion of perceiving all things to be separate.

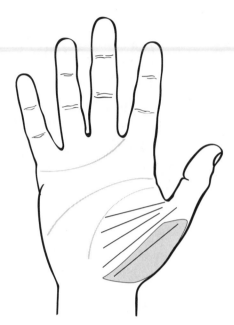

Figure 3.6—Worry lines in the area of the subconscious

These concepts also are fundamental to Zen Buddhism, as well as modern quantum physics.

Meister Eckhart emphasized the importance of becoming one with whatever is happening at the present moment. All things then become appreciated for their "beingness," free of any thoughts or perceptions we may try to project upon them. Detachment was important. In "On the Union with God," Eckhart writes, "You must know that to be empty of all created things is to be full of God, and that to be full of created things is to be empty of God."

As we delve into the region closest to the wrist (Figure 3.6), we begin to encounter worries that lurk below the threshold of conscious awareness. This is the area that records fear caused by our expectations.

Like fear, expectations exist only in our minds, yet what power they have! Either we fear a bad experience, or we yearn for something good to happen that may or may not happen. We also fear that our actions are unworthy; that we're a disappointment to other people. Some people play out "worst-case scenario" fantasies over and over in their minds, expecting the worst outcome of every situation. These expectations often keep us in a state of anxiety, and all over nothing more than a thought! Some of the symptoms of this are:

- A persistent feeling that nothing we do is good enough, that we aren't attractive, lovable, or competent, and that we don't deserve happiness or success.

- The belief that if people knew the true us, they wouldn't like us.

- Fear that what happiness we have will be taken from us to punish us for our shortcomings.

- Fear that if we lose control of a situation, it will annihilate us.

- Bottled-up resentment because we're afraid to speak our mind. In other words, our own needs aren't important enough to fight for.

- Fear of losing loved ones.

- Fear of commitment.

All of these attitudes are a result of placing too much importance on expectations—either those of ourselves or others. As children, we are burdened by the expectations of our parents to make them proud, by the expectations of our teachers to excel, and by the expectations of our peers to conform. Of course, we naturally want to please others, but if this desire becomes too driving a force, it can cause a lot of anxiety. I've lost count of the number of people whose palms I've read who are still trying to meet the expectations of parents long in the grave.

Probably the most crippling fear that falls within this area is the fear of failure. Of course, if we expect to fail, we probably will. Often we cannot face the possibility of success. Perhaps the demands made by achieving our dreams will be more than we can bear. We feel unworthy; that we lack the skills or the talent to be anything more than we are.

One cure for the fear of failure is to never try anything new or risky. The problem with this cure, however, is that you also deny yourself the rewards of success. It's a safe existence, but not very satisfying.

Plus, let's face it: great happiness is sometimes just as hard to withstand as great pain. Have you ever heard someone say that something was so exciting or joyful that "I couldn't stand it"? Most of us insulate ourselves from experiencing ecstasy by emotionally detaching. We watch our own lives pass by as though we were only observers. It takes practice to be happy!

The fear of failure is simply the flip side of the fear of success. To conquer the fear of failure we must first program ourselves for success. Don't listen to the negativity of others who have never tried anything risky. Seek out people who have accomplished what you want to accomplish and ask them how they did it. When you experience a temporary setback or disappointment, or when you fall short of perfection, don't dwell on the things you may have done wrong. Instead, concentrate on the things you did right. Over time, you'll see that the rewards of success will more than compensate for temporary setbacks and disappointments.

There's a very good reason why I've avoided the phrase "unrealistic expectations." From a karmic viewpoint, all expectations are unrealistic. Expectations are almost always a reflection of other people's views of how we should be. If we have difficulty meeting the expectations we set for ourselves, how much more difficult it is then to meet those projected upon us by other people! The important thing to remember is that another person's expectation is *their* karma, not ours.

Remember that karma begins with a mental, physical, or verbal action. Expectation is a mental action, therefore it sets into motion a karmic chain reaction. When we expect something to happen, we're setting up the possibility that it will not happen. Any disappointment we feel over our expectation's lack of fruition is the rebound effect of having the expectation in the first place. That particular karma begins and ends with us.

So, obviously we're under no moral obligation to meet the expectations projected upon us by others. If I were to ask you to fly around the room three times and perch on top of my microwave oven and you fail to do so, whose fault is that, yours or mine? Likewise, if your parents expect you to become a doctor or lawyer when your heart knows you should really be a sculptor or poet, the karma is not yours, but your parents' for trying to project their own expectations on to you. When someone says, "I'm disappointed in you," or "I expected better from you," the only sensible response is to realize that nobody has any business expecting *anything* from you. This isn't arrogance; it's just plain common sense.

THE PAIN OF CHANGE

It's hard to know what's good for us if we don't understand ourselves. As we mature and are affected by our experiences, traumas, joys, victories, and defeats, we become a complex mixture of who we really are and who we're expected to be. We set dreams aside in favor of the easily obtainable and less risky things in life. Our true identity becomes sublimated beneath the masks we're forced to wear. We may forget who we are, and what's really important to us.

I struggled for years trying to be an artist because teachers and family members told me I had a "talent" for it. Then I realized that no matter how long I went to school or how hard I tried, I just wasn't very good at it. No matter how skilled my paintings were technically, they just didn't have that mysterious something that grabs people by the gut and makes them pay attention. My work lacked passion. There was no emotional involvement between my work and the spectator. In fact, the only emotion I experienced while trying to create art was anxiety, which should have told me I was pursuing the wrong path. As Joseph Campbell reminded us, the secret of success is to follow our bliss. Anxiety certainly isn't bliss. After a long period of self-searching, I returned to the areas that made me happy: writing and performing. Change isn't easy, but it is necessary if we want to find out who we really are and what will make us happy.

Fear of change is universal and often paralyzing. We're challenged by the fear of losing loved ones, or of losing the comfort of our present circumstances. We're afraid to commit to relationships because we're afraid of a hurtful ending. This fear is magnified by the fairy-tale belief that a magical *something* can make our lives "happily ever after." If we don't find that "something," we think that we've failed at life.

Change is often difficult, but the fact is that if we do not change, we lose opportunities for growth. Perhaps the hardest lesson of all is that we must learn to accept the temporary nature of all things. *Everything* changes; this is the nature of life, and one of the most beautiful things about being a temporary creature. We have to accept that part of the old must die for a new *us* to appear. Members of our soul family come to us, teach us, and then move on once the work is completed. Clinging to relationships or situations whose time has passed is a sure way to set ourselves up for disappointment. We must learn to embrace the pain of change, or we'll lose the blessings and new opportunities that shifting circumstances create for us. Helen Keller once wrote, "Often we look so long at the closed door we fail to see the one that has opened for us." We can rest assured that the pain of change is quickly forgotten when the benefits appear.

WHEN WE DIE

Finally, we must address the biggest change of all: the transformation of flesh into spirit. Death frightens us because it is the Great Unknown, the Grim Reaper, the Dark Horseman, the Black Camel. Something extraordinary happens to us at the moment of death, but none of us are sure exactly what this something is, and that's what scares us the most. We hate going into a dark room.

In the final analysis, the fear of death is nothing more than an outgrowth of the fear of change. We're afraid that we'll lose our identity, our sense of self, all our nice stuff—the things that make us who we are. We fear that when we die it's the end of us, like a candle going out in the night. However, there is a large body of evidence to support that when we die, our consciousness continues to exist and can even interact with those still living.

As yet, there is no way to scientifically explore the world after death. Yet, according to those who have survived near-death experiences, all that happens to us when we die is a transformation into another state of being; a more stable, pure being of spiritual energy. In fact, the death process seems a lot like the birth process, but in reverse.

First, the soul begins to separate its connections to the physical body, one by one. We lose consciousness and drift off to sleep. We're not alone at the time of death; members of our soul family arrive to help us make the separation from our tired flesh. Eventually, we make our way through a long tunnel toward a Great Light where loved ones await us—a spiritual equivalent to our physical birth experience. Then, according to testimony retrieved under hypnotic past-life regressions, our souls enter a period of rejuvenation and rest where we're given advice and taught lessons from more advanced souls. When we're ready, we're then reborn as new, different people.

I must mention that skeptics, however, have constructed a different model of what happens to us as we die. Some psychologists have proposed that the near-death experience is nothing more than a hallucination experienced by a dying brain. According to this hypothesis, lack of oxygen causes the visual cortex of the brain to fire at random, which creates a tunnel-like effect. Furthermore, we experience the hallucinations of our loved ones as the consciousness slowly disintegrates. The brain tries to reconstruct events from our past and our memories arise at random.

If this scenario depresses you, you're not alone! I must point out that to date, there's no scientific proof that any of this actually happens, so we're still free to believe whatever we wish. Like the mullah in the story that prefaces this book, I have no desire to attempt to change the mindset of the world. However, personally, I believe the evidence of reincarnation far outweighs any other theory of what happens to us after we die. So for the purposes of this book, we'll stick with the reincarnation idea. We die and move out of our body like a hermit crab abandoning its shell.

Where this is interesting to palmists is that after the death of the physical body, all the lines in our hands gradually disappear except the head, heart, and life lines—the ones we started with in the womb. Over time, these three lines fade away too. Eventually, if we so decide, we'll be reborn as a new, different person with an entirely new set of circumstances and challenges to occupy our attention.

THE SAME, ONLY DIFFERENT

As we've seen, we're an amalgamation of all the lives we've ever lived. As Buddha pointed out, our myriad reincarnations are like the flickering of a candle's flame: not the same flame by any means, nor is it a different flame. Just as the adult we are today both is and isn't the same as the baby we were at birth, so it is when we die. Death is simply a rebirth into another existence. Exploring those other existences can give us many insightful clues into why we are the way we are.

Past-Life Regression: The Christos Method

A valuable technique for exploring past lives is called the Christos technique. In my experience, this powerful visualization technique almost never fails.

It all started in the early seventies—that romantic and scintillating era—when a hypnotist named Jaquelin Parkhurst published an article titled "The Christos Experience." The article described a hypnotic procedure that proved useful in creating lucid dreams. Impressed with this method, Australian author G. L. Glaskin went on to write several books on using the Christos method to help clients experience past lives. I will describe the Christos method and then add some of my own variations.

The subject lies on his back with a cushion comfortably supporting his head. The hypnotist vigorously massages the third-eye area of the forehead, or the crown chakra. Parkhurst suggests that at the same time a helper should massage the subject's feet and ankles (I personally have never tried this part).

The subject is then told to imagine himself growing two inches taller through the soles of his feet, and then shrinking back to his previous state. He is told to repeat this procedure with his head—expanding two inches and then returning. This visualization is repeated several times with the stretching extended to twelve inches, then to two feet. Then the subject is asked to imagine himself expanding like a balloon in every direction until he begins to float.

Next the subject is told to visualize his front door and to describe it in detail. Then he imagines himself on the roof of his house and describes everything he sees.

Now for the crucial phase of this fascinating method: the subject is asked to ascend five hundred feet into the air and to visualize himself floating above the earth, slowly drifting like a cloud. This scene is described by the subject, both by night and by day. Then, when he is ready, he is to slowly descend to the earth. I add, "And as you descend to the earth, you will enter one of your past lives; one of your choice."

When he lands, the subject is asked to imagine that he is looking at his feet in his past life and to describe them. He is to describe himself and what he is wearing. He will always see himself as changed. He may find himself in another life at another time. The average time for this induction can be from ten to twenty minutes.

I have a couple of variations to this that I have found to be effective. At the very beginning of the procedure while the client is starting to relax, I ask him to open his chakras one by one as he exhales. I touch him on the crown of his head and say, "Take a deep breath and exhale, and as you do, imagine the top of your head opening. Open the chakra, letting the light in. Deep breath [*touching the forehead*], exhale, and open your third eye. Open, open wide, wide open."

I repeat this touching and breathing procedure with the other chakras, one by one. I do not touch the chakras below the belly button, but ask the person to visualize and open them. Then I proceed with the "growing two inches" visualization.

When the subject opens his imaginary eyes and describes his feet as wearing sandals or boots, I begin questioning him about the past existence. I take the person through various important episodes of his past life, just as you might with someone interesting you have just met. I continually insist on details, and continually ask the person to describe his feelings at the time of the event.

The final scenario I ask the subject to describe is the manner of his death. Invariably the person describes the actual death process as a peaceful and relaxed experience. As the subject's spirit leaves the body from the past life, I ask him to return to floating above the earth. Then, when he is ready, I ask him to return to the current time and place and open his eyes.

The steps to ensure a successful regression are:

- Plant positive affirmations from the outset to encourage anticipation of success.

- Discuss the theory of past lives, why we have them, and what we learn from them.

- Engage the individual in a series of visualization exercises.

To expand on the last point: when the person enters the past life, ask a lot of questions about the past life to aid the participant in remembering details. Ask the person frequently to express the feelings associated with the people, places, and events he describes. This ensures that the subject will have emotional involvement in the experience, which makes for a richer and more satisfying regression.

Usually, the subject will remember more and more detail in days to come whenever he thinks about the experience. Ask your subject what karmic lessons he has brought into this life from the past life experience. Sometimes it's helpful after the subject enters a past life to go on and say, "Now, look to your right, and you will see me there, in the role I served in my past life. Describe me as you see me in this place and time." This can give the subject a secure feeling; he has a friend and guide on the other side.

Past-Life Regression: On Your Own

The Christos method can also be used by yourself. Simply find a room where you can relax without fear of interruption. Dim the lights, relax deeply in a comfortable chair or bed, and follow the procedure outlined above.

The lesson we learn from the exploration of our past lives is that rather than fearing death, we should look forward to the opportunity to enter a better existence. We assure this better existence through acts of compassion and charity, and by becoming the totality of our potential—the person we were destined to be. We give our gifts back to the world and thus pay the Universe back for our life.

> *How can I tell if love of life is a delusion?*
>
> *How can I know that a man who fears death is not like a man who has left home and dreads returning?*
>
> *How can I tell whether the dead are not amazed that they ever clung to life?*
>
> —Chuang Tsu, *Inner Chapters*

chapter four

KARMA & HEALTH

Life is suffering.

—Siddhartha Gautama, the Buddha

Pain is Inevitable; Suffering is Optional.

—Sylvia Boorstein, *That's Funny,*
You Don't Look Buddhist

*I*n a moment we will discuss some of the clues the hand can give us about
our health. Before we do, I must make one point perfectly clear: *palm read-*
ers and other psychics should not practice medicine or give a medical diagnosis unless
they are qualified to do so.

Several years ago I used to work the psychic fair circuit. Psychic fairs are sort of
metaphysical trade shows. They are usually held in hotels where psychic readers sit
at tables and give short readings for a small fee. It's a great way for people to get a lot
of readings for comparison, but you cannot always be sure that you're getting a reliable psychic. Although most psychic fair promoters are very careful whom they
allow to attend, sometimes—pardon the expression—a few fruitcakes manage to
sneak in.

Most experienced psychics avoid giving advice in the legal, financial, and medical fields, but at a few of the fairs I attended, I overheard psychics dispensing medical advice right and left. One day I was horrified to hear a little grandmotherly lady being advised by a psychic to throw away her heart medicine. "You don't need that," the psychic told her. "Doctors don't know what they're doing." After the reading I took the elderly woman aside and advised her not to throw her medicine away. Fortunately, the woman had the good sense not to take the psychic's advice. However, others may have been so impressed by the psychic that they would have readily complied, and suffered the consequences.

So, on the subject of medical diagnosis, don't do it. With that caution firmly in mind, let's take a look at medical palmistry.

ATTITUDE IS EVERYTHING

When the worry lines attack the life line, it represents psychosomatic reactions that may affect the person's health or physical vitality (Figure 4.1). When the lines get this far, stress-related illness, fatigue, and depression may not be far behind. When the body experiences stress, it activates our primal fight-or-flight mechanism. The heart races and adrenaline floods the bloodstream as we prepare for crisis. If the stress is unresolved over long periods of time, it puts a lot of wear and tear on the body. Long periods of stress can carve vertical lines in the phalanges of the fingers (Figure 4.2) called strain lines. The lines in the first phalanx take weeks to carve, lines in the middle phalanx take months, and by the time they reach the fingertips, it represents years of stress. If unrelenting stress can affect the fingers so dramatically, just imagine what must be going on in other parts of the body (the heart muscles and arteries, for example).

Furthermore, researchers at Liverpool University have discovered that men with extralong ring fingers are more likely to suffer from depression than other men. If a person's ring finger is much longer than his forefinger, you would expect a greater likelihood of depression.

We know that attitude and mental state can have a direct, powerful bearing on our health, so it's important to eliminate any negative mental karma that could come back to harm us. A strong example of the power of attitude can be found in

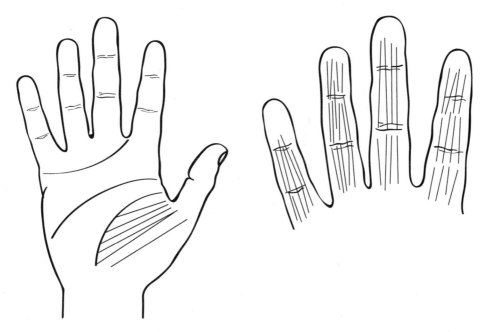

Figures 4.1 and 4.2—Worry lines attacking the life line (left) and strain lines (right)

the *AHHA Guide to Alternative Medicine*, reported by Dr. Bruno Klopfer in the *Journal of Projective Techniques* in 1957.

A man with metastatic cancer had tumors that had spread throughout his body. The patient had tried every available form of medicine and his condition had hopelessly deteriorated to the point where he was bedridden and gasping for air. Then the man heard about an experimental drug called Krebiozin, and insisted on being included in the experimental trials. His doctors, feeling he had nothing to lose, agreed to give him the experimental drug. To their amazement, the man's tumors began to shrink dramatically and he was discharged from the hospital.

Two months later, the man read news accounts of the research on Krebiozin that reported serious doubts with the drug. Within a matter of days, the man's tumors had returned and were again threatening his life. His doctor cleverly convinced him that a new and more potent shipment had been received and proceeded to give him injections of plain water. His tumors once again began to shrink dramatically. He remained healthy for several more months until another news report declared that Krebiozin was worthless as a cancer treatment.

The man died within two days.

This is a chilling scenario. Are we killing ourselves with our own negativity? Stress is definitely bad karma.

REFUSING TO PLAY THE STRESS GAME

Remember, it isn't the stress that affects us but how we react to it. There are many effective techniques to help us relax and reduce the amount of stress we carry with us. Below is a description of a Zen technique called Void Meditation. I like it because it uses the hands as a central focus. Void Meditation not only relieves stress, but it also increases mental clarity, improves digestion, and reduces joint pain.

To begin, sit comfortably and place your hands together, palm to palm. Interlock your fingers, and then extend the two forefingers. The forefingers should point upward toward the sky, the tips about even with your breastbone. Extend the thumbs at right angles to the forefingers (Figure 4.3).

Now, separate the forefingers about an inch apart. Stare into the "void" between the fingertips and imagine them moving together. Amazingly, your forefingers will be pulled toward each other as though they were magnetic.

As soon as the fingertips touch, take a deep breath and hold your hands near your chest, elbows relaxed naturally at your side. Your thumbs should be pointing at your heart. Feel the palm-to-palm contact of your hands; sense the pulse between your palms. Keep your attention focused on the point where your forefinger tips touch. Breathe deeply and in a relaxed manner. Do not try to stop the thoughts that naturally enter and leave your mind, but notice the spaces or "void" between the thoughts. Recognizing and extending this void is the purpose of this meditation. The more you can maintain this void, the more relaxed you will become.

More Stress-beating Strategies

Reflexology techniques can help reduce specific symptoms of stress on a short-term basis. An easy stress symptom to alleviate is neck tension. Grasp your thumb

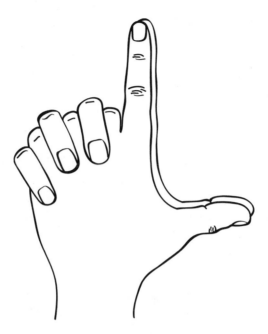

Figure 4.3—Void Meditation

(or better yet, get a friend to do it) and rotate the tip gently side to side several times on both knuckles. Repeat on the other hand until your neck relaxes. If tension hits you in the lower back, gently massage the center of the wrist on the palm side with the opposite thumb. Massage each wrist for five minutes, several times a day, until the backache disappears.

If you suffer from stress headaches, massage the thumbs. Start at the pad on the tip of the thumb and gently massage toward the knuckle. Locate any points that feel sore and rub these spots thoroughly. If your headache still persists after massaging the first phalanx, move to the second phalanx and repeat the process. If necessary, also rub the web of the thumb and the metacarpal bone. Headaches around the eyes require massaging the index and middle fingers. Headaches around the ears will need additional manipulation of the ring and little fingers. Obviously, if the headache is on the right side, concentrate the treatment on the right hand. For headaches on the left side, use the left hand.

If you like this sort of stuff (and personally, I love it), there's a lot more useful information on the connection between palmistry, the chakras, and reflexology in chapter 7.

PHYSICAL CONDITIONS AND KARMA

Some schools of thought believe that handicaps and health problems are caused by karma. For example, if you have asthma, it could be because you were responsible for somebody drowning or suffocating in a previous life. I'm not convinced that this is the case. The concept that past suffering can be balanced by present suffering smacks of revenge and the concept of payback—how can two wrongs make a right? I prefer to think that a chronic illness teaches us to develop our inner resources. Dealing with a chronic condition such as asthma, diabetes, or arthritis requires diligence, love, discipline, and patience. Most physical obstacles aren't insurmountable, but seem to be designed to test our determination. We can learn a lot from the example of Helen Keller. She was born blind, deaf, and mute, and overcame her handicaps to become an inspiration to not only those born with sensory impairments, but to us all. Sometimes hardship and misfortune bring out the nobility in us.

Pretty much everybody knows that high blood pressure can be detected by redness near the base of the nailbed, and that asthma or emphysema can turn the flesh under the nail a bluish color. Yet the nails are also one of the first places a doctor can find the early signs of jaundice and gall bladder or liver disease. For example, Hippocratic or "watch-glass" nails, which are round, bluish, and shiny (Figure 4.4) can indicate cirrhosis of the liver, tuberculosis, and chronic heart disease. If I saw these on a subject, I would recommend he or she visit a doctor for a complete checkup.

According to some palmists, glandular imbalances can be identified from lines upon the tips of the fingers. In my experience, these signs aren't always true, but they are usually right more often than not. Therefore they can still be considered useful. Strong diagonal lines or a grille formation found on any fingertip reveals a glandular problem. The deeper the lines, the more severe the condition. Each fingertip relates to a different gland as follows:

- Index finger—pituitary gland

- Middle finger—adrenal glands

Figures 4.4 and 4.5—A "watch-glass" nail (left) and a nail scooping inward (right)

- Third finger—thymus gland

- Little finger—thyroid gland

When the grille formation is found on every finger, the most common cause is menopause, or an adverse reaction to birth control medication.

An overactive thyroid can sometimes be spotted if the nails scoop inward or have strong horizontal ridges (Figure 4.5). An underactive thyroid can sometimes be spotted by thin, brittle-ridged, and exceptionally short nails, especially if the nail's "moon" is missing.

Heart disease is often accompanied by a clubbing of the fingertips (Figure 4.6) and a bluish tinge to the fingernails. Small nodules beneath the skin near the heart line can indicate that the person has had a heart attack, or even a "silent" heart attack. These are detected by pressing the skin. They feel like hard little BBs under the flesh.

A rather alarming sign is the presence of *palmar keratoses*, which may indicate cancer. These are yellowish, platelike scales, usually few in number, that appear on the Mount of Venus or the Mount of Luna (Figure 4.7). According to Dr. Eugene Scheimann, M.D., these keratoses were found in 45 percent of patients diagnosed with cancer in a study by Dr. R. L. Dobson in *Archives of Dermatology*, November 1965.*

---

*Eugene Scheimann, M.D., *A Doctor's Guide to Better Health Through Palmistry* (West Nyack, N.Y.: Parker Publishing Company, 1969), 55–58.

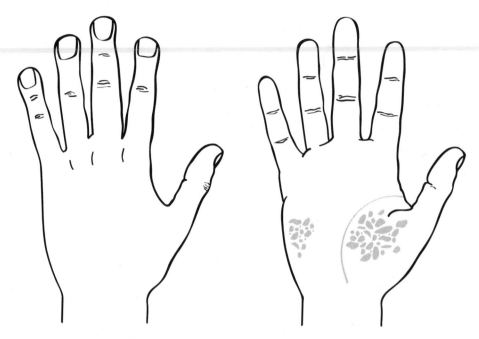

Figures 4.6 and 4.7—Clubbed fingertips (left) and palmar keratoses (right)

Rheumatoid arthritis and osteoarthritis can be spotted by the swelling of a finger's first knuckle (the knuckle between the first and second phalanges). The knuckle will begin to enlarge long before there are other physical symptoms of arthritis. According to some palmists, the part of the body affected is shown by a knuckle enlargement of the corresponding finger:

- Index finger—hips and lower back

- Middle finger—knees

- Third finger—legs and feet

- Little finger—neck and upper back

Once again, these signs are not graven in stone. Yet they are true more often than not, and are useful as early-warning signs that may indicate a physical checkup is necessary.

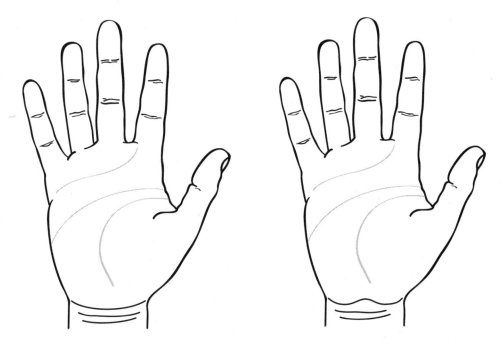

Figures 4.8 and 4.8A—Rascettes (left) and an upward curve of the top rascette (right)

Most people have one or more rascettes or bracelets at the point where the bottom of the hand joins the wrist (Figure 4.8). When there are two or more bracelets, it gives extra assurance that the person will be alert and active in his or her old age.

The rascettes are at their most powerful when they take the form of a smooth curve. However, when the top rascette curves upward into the palm on a woman's hand (Figure 4.8A), it can mean that she will have gynecological difficulties or problems during childbirth.

FIRST, DO NO HARM!

So what do you do if you notice any of these signs in your palm, or in the palm of someone for whom you are reading? *Do not jump to conclusions, and by no means should you diagnose!* Instead, go to the doctor (or advise your subject to go to the doctor) for a checkup before you jump to conclusions. These are potential early warning signs, but they may be caused by other factors. Do not plant negative seeds of anxiety in your subject's mind. Reread the Krebiozin story at the beginning of this chapter, and use extreme caution.

So what good does this information do us if we can't diagnose? As I pointed out, sometimes it can act as an early warning and we can refer someone to a doctor in time to alleviate the illness.

Let me tell you a story. One time at a county fair I was reading a woman's hands and noticed small red lines in several of her fingernails. These are called "splinter hemorrhages" and indicate the presence of a parasitic spirochete. I asked her if she felt tired and listless lately. "Lord bless you, yes," she said, sighing. "I'm just worn out. The doctor doesn't know what to do with me." I asked her if she handled raw meat. Surprised, she said that she worked on a pig farm on the weekends packaging freshly slaughtered pork.

"Go back to your doctor and tell him you suspect you have trichinosis," I told her, writing the word down on a piece of paper. Trichinosis is a rather nasty parasite, and well-known in the South, which you can pick up from handling raw pork. The splinter hemorrhages are the body's attempt to expel the parasite through the nail beds. I picked up this little bit of trivia from a dermatology textbook that dealt with medical conditions recognized through the fingernails.

About six months later I saw the woman at a company picnic and asked her how she was feeling. "Great!" she said, waving a chili-laden hotdog in the air. She had taken my advice and asked her doctor to check her for trichinosis. When he found it, he asked her how she figured it out. "I told him that my psychic told me!" she said. Now, I know better than to wish to be an animal or insect, but just that once I wish I could have been a fly on the doctor's wall when she said that.

Some say the nimble-witted Mercury
Went late disguised professing palmistry,
And Milk-maid's fortunes told about the
*   Land,*
Only to get a touch of her soft hand.

—William Browne, "Cheiromancy"

chapter five

INDIAN
THUMB READING

Every soul is a melody which needs renewing.

—Stéphane Mallarmé, *To Purify the
Words of the Tribe*

*U*nfortunately, the origin of palmistry is so obscured by time (not to mention
a great deal of false information and creative romanticizing) that it is impossible to determine where the practice first began. As Fred Gettings points out in
The Book of the Hand, "There is no palmistry [as a codified science], only palmists."

However hard it is to track, palmistry is generally agreed to have its roots in the
East. The earliest records referring to palmistry come from India, where it is
believed that palmistry was given to humans as a gift from Samudra, the ocean
god. From India, the practice gained acceptance in Greece and Egypt, and eventually trickled to the rest of the world. Certain aspects of Indian palmistry were preserved and spread throughout Europe by the Gypsies who left India in the thir-
teenth century.

When Kasimir D'Arpentigny (considered the father of modern scientific palmistry) began systematically recording information about hand reading in the

nineteenth century, he received a great deal of data from a young Gypsy woman. He wrote that although a fair amount of the woman's discourse was, in his opinion, nonsense, he nonetheless sensed that the terminology preserved the remnants of a forgotten language—the language of the hand.

THE THUMB: MASTER OF THE HAND

Indian palmists divide their craft into three categories: *darsana* (seeing), which is the analysis of the hand's color; *sparsana* (touching), which concentrates on the texture and temperature of the hand; and *rekha vimarsana*, which involves reading the lines and symbols of the hand.

One of the major differences between Indian palmistry and Western palmistry is that many Indian palmists concern themselves mainly with reading the thumb. In *Your Destiny in Thumb*, the author R. G. Rao maintains that an individual's entire destiny and personality can be determined from a study of the thumb alone. This isn't surprising. After all, the thumb is the most important digit on the hand, occupying far more area than any of the other fingers. Without the thumb, the rest of the fingers are pretty much helpless. As the visible representation of our logic, will power, and passion, it can truly be said that the thumb is the master of the hand.

Like their Western counterparts, Indian hand readers test the thumb for stiffness by flexing it toward the wrist (Figure 5.1). If the thumb is firm, it shows determination and will power. If totally inflexible, it shows a very stubborn person; someone with whom it may be a little hard to get along.

However, if the thumb is weak and easily bent, the person will be generous, broad-minded, and polite. On the negative side, the person with a weak thumb may have problems standing up to other people. Often, this person is quite likely to give in to the demands of others.

A firm and flexible thumb is the ideal balance between the two extremes. Such a person, according to Rao, will ". . . walk slow, will do any work undertaken with due care and foresight; though a little hasty, will immediately mend any mistakes committed . . . and acquire scholarship in any subject."[†] The person

---

†R. G. Rao, *Your Destiny in Thumb* (New Delhi, India: Ranjan Publications, 1983), 11.

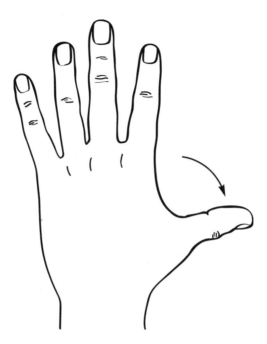

Figure 5.1—Testing the thumb for flexibility

with such a "Sword Thumb" will be socially flexible, adaptive, able to take control when necessary, but not driven by the desire to always be the boss. Remember, in palmistry, as well as karma, balance is everything.

THE HORIZONTAL REKHAS OF THE THUMB

Figure 5.2 shows the nine major lines, or *rekhas*, of the thumb. Not everyone will have all of these lines; in fact, it will be a very rare individual who has them all. On the palmar side of the thumb are rekhas that indicate important karmic events. We will begin with the horizontal rekhas.

The Pushpa Rekha

The line separating the first phalanx (Rhea) from the second (Athena) is called the *pushpa rekha*, or the *wheat line* (also known as the *phela rekha*; line A). If the line is firm and clear, it means you will always have enough to eat. It's especially

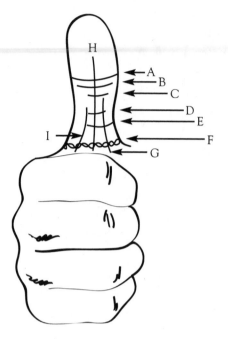

Figure 5.2—The rekhas of the thumb

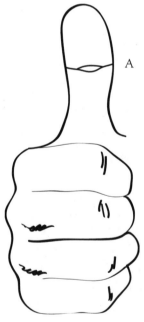

Figure 5.3—A "grain of rice" in the pushpa rekha

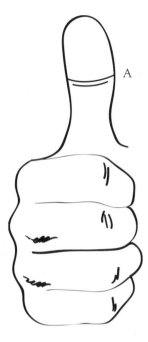

Figure 5.4—The wheat line's male and female lines

fortunate to have what appears to be a grain of wheat or rice in it (Figure 5.3). This is reassuring in countries such as India and China where, even today, poverty is common. In prosperous countries it doesn't carry quite as much karmic impact, but it does assure the owner that he or she will have the basic necessities of life, no matter how bad times may get.

More than any other line on the thumb, the wheat line is linked to karma. It follows the owner's *purva karma* (actions in the previous birth), and its presence quite candidly reflects the good and bad results of the person's past life. According to ancient tradition, a good wheat line predicts longevity.

The wheat line often consists of two lines: male and female (Figure 5.4). On a man's hand, the subsidiary line is called the *stri rekha* (woman's line), and on a woman's hand it is the *purusa rekha* (man's line). If this subsidiary line is broken, it indicates frequent disturbances in the family. Black dots on the subsidiary line shows a wasting away of money. In other words, that particular relationship will cost you! It can also indicate outliving the marital partner.

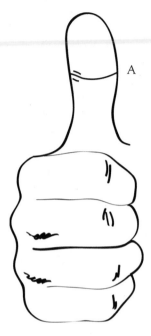

Figure 5.5—A dented wheat line

If the subsidiary line begins early near the wheat line, the person will probably start a family early. This may not be as true today in this era of planned parenthood as it was a hundred years ago, but I've found it happens often enough to justify the interpretation.

If the subsidiary lines are numerous, the person will have many liaisons.

If the wheat line is broken or dented (Figure 5.5), it predicts a period of time when the owner will have to struggle to make ends meet. The timing of this can be predicted by the appearance of the wheat line. If the line is dented at the beginning (the side nearest the wrist) and smooth for the rest of its length, the person will have a troubled childhood, but things get better over time. If the dents are in the middle of the line, it indicates a period of hardship in midlife. If the dented area is at the end of the wheat line, it predicts problems in old age, which the person will have to provide for through investment and saving money.

The Madhura Rekha

Just beneath the wheat line one sometimes finds a line called the *madhura rekha* (Figure 5.2, line B), which gives the owner a liberal, charitable disposition. It could well be called the humanitarian line for this reason.

The Mandara Rekha

Next is the line known as the *mandara rekha* (Figure 5.2, line C), which represents travel. People with this line will have a restless nature, love to go on trips, and have a strong dislike for restrictions and limitations. If forced by circumstances to suppress their wandering spirit, they learn to travel in their minds, and get a vicarious satisfaction from watching movies or reading books about exotic places. They can be spectacular daydreamers.

The Mana Rekha

Occasionally you will find a line like line D in Figure 5.2, which is called the *mana rekha*. If found on a man's hand, he is likely to be tempted to have extramarital affairs. If he overcomes temptation, he will still be thinking about it a lot, or "lusting in the heart." On a woman's hand it can mean the same, however, it can also mean she will have a lot of male friends. I've often found the mana on the hands of women who are close friends with one or more gay men.

Sexual temptation is one of our more difficult karmic tests to resist. It is said that, during his period of meditation under the Bhodhi tree, which led to his enlightenment, Buddha was tempted with wealth, social standing, and sexual pleasure.

The Rathi Rekha

The *rathi* (or *mohini*) *rekha* (Figure 5.2, line E) is one of the most complicated lines of the thumb. It contains a great deal of information concerning the marriage lines (see the discussion of lines of karmic connection in the next chapter), and must be compared to the marriage lines to determine the nature of the relationship. Rathi is read as follows:

- If the rathi has a small island, the person will be in a relationship where he or she will have to take care of the other partner for a period of time, thus learning the karmic lesson of healing. Traditionally, this has meant that the person's romantic partner will be physically ill, but I've also seen the rathi island on the hands of people whose spouses were recovering alcoholics or drug addicts, suffering from depression or anxiety disorders, or other emotional or mental problems. They may have to face the death of their marital partner at some point in their life.

- In conjunction with a chained or broken wheat line, the person may remarry several times.

- If the rathi is cut in half by a small line, relationship problems begin in midlife, usually with the illness of the partner.

- A severely broken or dotted rathi indicates a "lone wolf," or someone who prefers a solitary lifestyle.

The Malika Rekha

The *malika rekha* (Figure 5.2, line F) looks like a chain of flowers that divides the phalanx of Athena from the Mount of Venus. In India, the malika is a small white flower that is offered to Lord Siva. In Western palmistry, the malika rekha is sometimes called the family line and indicates that home and hearth is dear to the person's heart. It means the same in Indian palmistry, assuming the line is clear and well marked, and that the person's family life will be a happy one. Dots on the malika rekha indicate financial squabbles within the family, and quite often I've verified that the dots indicate someone in the family who stole or cheated money away from the others. If the malika is noticeably bolder than the wheat line, the person will have problems sustaining relationships, usually because of an extremely close attachment to the parents.

THE VERTICAL REKHAS OF THE THUMB

Now we must look for vertical lines that run the length of the thumb. Although some thumbs have numerous lines that run its length, Indian palmistry recognizes

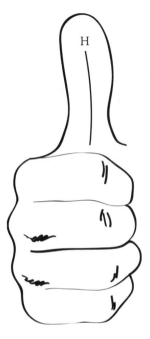

Figure 5.6—The mangala rekha

only three of these to have significance: the kasara, mangala, and vajra rekhas (Figure 5.2, lines G, H, and I). The others are companion, sister, or subsidiary lines.

The Mangala Rekha

The line that rises from the Mount of Venus and divides the thumb in half is called the *mangala* (or *repu*) *rekha* (Figure 5.2, line H, or Figure 5.6). The mangala represents enemies or other adversarial forces, which is why it is also called the repu rekha, since the word *repu* means "enemy" or "opponent." Any of the horizontal lines discussed above that the mangala cuts will have its beneficial powers weakened.

The Vajra Rekha

On the side of the thumb nearest the fingers you will sometimes find a vertical line called the *vajra rekha* or the *diamond line* (Figure 5.2, line I). It conveys a

mixed blessing: the person may enjoy money, success, and other worldly pleasures, but suffer from physical or mental illness or addiction. This is because the
person may lose sight of the important things in life. No amount of success or
wealth can appease the spirit's longing to rid itself from the burden of karmic
debt. If we're not diligently working toward becoming the sum of our potential,
we're not learning the karmic lessons we must learn. We'll feel a nagging inside
our spirit; a restlessness, depression, and a lack of direction. We'll lose our sense of
purpose, which is why job burnout is so common the malady has been described
as an epidemic. There's a lot more to life than fame and wealth. As an old Italian
proverb points out, "Once the game is over, the king and the pawn go back into
the same box."

If the line is clear (Figure 5.7), it indicates great wealth; if faint, it shows a
more moderate—but still impressive—prosperity. Yet always keep in mind that
the person must be careful not to neglect his or her health as he or she chases the
big bucks.

The Kasara Rekha

On the opposite side of the thumb is the *kasara rekha* (Figure 5.2, line G), which
represents the gradual rise of the person's family circumstances. When it is very
fine and difficult to detect, it indicates that the family will build its wealth gradually over time, sometimes taking generations to reach prosperity. A thicker, bolder
line means the person will come into money fairly quickly (Figure 5.8). It can
presage a lottery win or insurance settlement—a windfall. If we're tempted to
think that winning a lottery isn't an enormous challenge, look at the number of
people whose lives are literally ruined by the sudden acquisition of wealth. (In
"Lottery Win Can Cause Headaches," which appeared in the *CNEWS* magazine
dated December 2, 2001, journalist Tim Cook documented several examples of
people whose lives were upset by sizable lottery wins.) However, if the windfall is
treated with wisdom and respect, it can be a wonderful blessing.

I witnessed the most dramatic example of this latter phenomenon about a year
ago. A middle-aged carpenter had come to me for advice about starting his own
business. Unfortunately, he had no money for start-up funds. I looked at his
kasara and noticed that it suddenly grew thicker past the halfway point. "I think

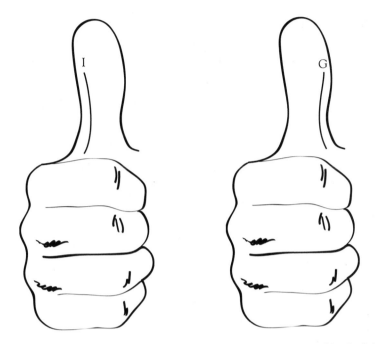

Figures 5.7 and 5.8—A clear vajra rekha (left) and the kasara rekha (right)

you will probably come into some money fairly soon," I told him. "Probably from a source unknown to you at this time." He was a bit skeptical, but about a month later he called me with good news. His wife was watching a television program that located missing people. Among the segments was a story about unclaimed inheritance money. A list of names was displayed on the screen, and as it turned out, the carpenter's wife was a missing heiress! It wasn't a huge amount of money, but it was more than enough for her husband to start his business. I enjoyed a happy result as well. The carpenter, with an innate understanding of the law of karma, insisted on fixing my old front porch free of charge.

Indian palmists also examine the thumb for figures of fish, scorpions, cobras, conch shells, wheels, and so on; all of which have certain specific meanings. A list of all the possible shapes and configurations would fill a book twice this size. They also carefully examine the thumb print for signs and portents, which is an application of the branch of hand reading known as *dermatoglyphics*. If you're interested in pursuing this fascinating branch of hand reading, I've recommended some sources in the bibliography. For now, let's leave the thumb and turn our attention to the most satisfying and sometimes exasperating source of our karmic experience: our soul mates.

Beware lest you lose the substance
by grasping at the shadow!

—Aesop, *The Complete Fables*

chapter six

THE KARMIC FAMILY

I am the family face;
Flesh perishes, I live on,
Projecting trait and trace
Through time to times anon,
And leaping from place to place
Over oblivion.

—Thomas Hardy, *Thomas Hardy:*
The Complete Poems

Fortunately, we're not alone as we face life's challenges. We are helped by members of our soul family, both spiritual and physical. Our soul families existed long before we were born into this world, and they will continue to be with us throughout eternity.

What are soul families? Research into past-life dynamics reveals that we often encounter the same people again and again throughout our numerous lifetimes. These people take on the roles of friends, family members, and romantic partners—in other words, soul mates. Groups of soul mates seem to travel together throughout eternity, and form soul families. Everyone is a member of a soul family, and even pets and guardian spirits are part of our families. In any given lifetime, some members of

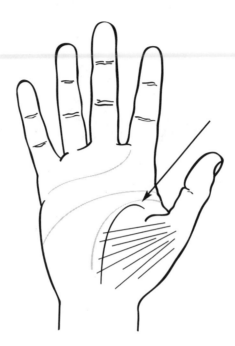

Figure 6.1—Line of protection

our soul family are in flesh while others are in spirit, but all can be counted on to help us when we need them.

SIGNS OF PROTECTION

We've already examined how to read worry lines as a model of our karmic debt. Occasionally, we'll see smaller, secondary lines running parallel to the life line. These are traditionally called *family lines* or *lines of protection* (Figure 6.1), and indicate a protective influence. Notice how these lines form a barrier that blocks some of the worry lines from reaching the life line. This is a clear and graphic illustration of the protective influences in our lives, such as guardian spirits, angels, and soul mates who are in spirit.

Often these lines represent "near misses"—times when we were snatched from the jaws of danger through spiritual intervention. Protective spirits are usually with us when we're in a potentially hazardous situation, like driving a car. Have you ever had a sudden feeling to pull off the road, or to go home by an alternate route, only to find out later that if you had ignored the feeling you would have been involved in a wreck? My friend Craig Karges (who is a professional mind reader) shares this story from his book *The Wizard's Legacy: A Tale of Real Magic*:

A couple of months after the . . . party I was driving late at night through the Southeast. I had a show at the University of Tennessee in Knoxville the following afternoon and I wanted to get there in time to grab a full night's sleep. I encountered a patch of heavy fog on the highway. The fog was so dense in places I literally couldn't see three feet in front of my hood. It was as though the entire world had vanished, leaving me alone in a cloud of white mist. I slowed down to avoid rear-ending any car that might be in front of me. I wasn't too worried, though. I was less than an hour away from Knoxville and making good time.

Suddenly the fog lifted just enough for me to see a lone figure standing on the side of the road, an old man dressed in black. His face was very pale. My breath caught in my throat. *God,* I thought, *that old guy better get off the road. Someone's going to hit him!* I saw him for just an instant, a photo-flash of recognition, and then I drove past him.

Doc? I thought.

I looked in the rear view mirror, but the fog had closed back again like a thick curtain. I was uncomfortably reminded of the dream I had the night Doc died, where I saw him disappear into a similar fog. *Don't be silly,* I reminded myself. *The old man wasn't Doc. He couldn't have been Doc.* I'd just imagined that he looked like him.

Nevertheless, a feeling of apprehension came over me. The thought entered my mind that I should pull off the highway and stop for the night. Something just didn't feel right. I pulled off the next exit and checked into a hotel in Dayton, Tennessee. I was extremely tired and fell asleep almost immediately.

The next morning I awoke refreshed and went down into the hotel restaurant, feeling a little foolish for overreacting the night before. The fog had lifted and a beautiful day greeted me. Over a cup of coffee I picked up the newspaper and saw the headline:

Forty Car Pileup on I-75 Kills 25.

Stunned, I read the details. Apparently, a tractor-trailer had collided with a slow-moving car just a couple of miles from the exit where I had decided to pull off for the night. Due to the extremely poor visibility, the initial wreck caused a chain reaction involving forty vehicles. Thirty-four people were injured and twenty-five died in the tragic accident. If I hadn't pulled off when I did, I might have been one of them.

I didn't know what to think. Was that solitary figure standing on the shoulder of that foggy Tennessee highway Doc, trying to catch my attention and warn me? Or was it just some poor old man wandering around on the side of the road?

Doc was Craig's great-uncle; a retired psychic with whom Craig had spent a period of time in apprenticeship in his childhood. This example illustrates how our loved ones often act as spiritual guardians—their love for us outlives the death of the physical body. However, rarely do our guardian spirits act so directly. Usually, their help is more subtle. Many people have stories about a time when they were driving somewhere and suddenly had the insistent urge to pull off the road. Others have said they were on the way home and decided suddenly to go via an alternate route. Often, people who report these experiences say they discovered later that they had avoided a wreck or natural disaster. If this has happened to you, it could have been your guardian whispering to you to watch out for yourself.

Lines that fork off from the beginning of the life line (like in Figure 6.1) indicate a human spirit; someone who may have taken care of you before he or she passed on, and who still watches after you in spirit.

Large, free-floating lines (Figure 6.2) on the other hand, indicate angelic protection; what is commonly known as having a guardian angel. Soul families seem to have specific guardian angels assigned to them as mentors and teachers.

Small curved lines (Figure 6.3) are usually the spirits of former pets and other protective animal spirits. Sometimes they can indicate the spirits of children, but we usually look under the little finger for children lines, both physical and spiritual. We'll discuss children lines shortly.

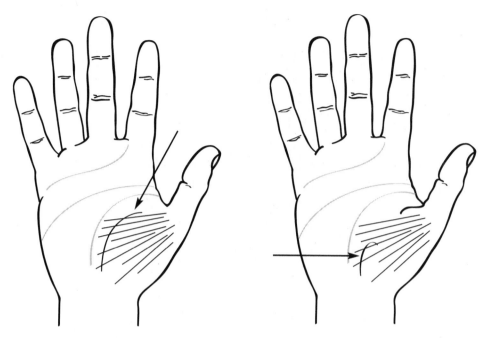

Figures 6.2 and 6.3—Line of angelic protection (left) and small line of protection (right)

MARRIAGE LINES

What about our living soul mates, the ones with whom we form friendships, marriages, and other physical relationships; those special people with whom we laugh, make love, and learn about ourselves? Once again, classical palmistry gives us a hint. On the edge of the hand, just beneath the little finger, are horizontal lines known in classical palmistry as marriage lines (Figure 6.4). Not so long ago, it was believed that these lines predicted the number of times a person would be married. This legend is so persistent that even today, many palmists from the old school read them this way.

However, experience has shown that the predictive quality of these lines (at least as far as the number of marriages is concerned) is not as infallible as we would like. Because of changing times and a more relaxed moral atmosphere, modern palmists redefined the marriage lines as lines of commitment or relationship, and use them to predict the number of emotionally important love affairs. Unfortunately, exactly

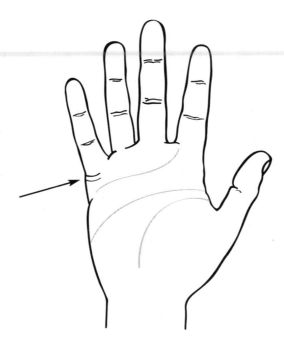

Figure 6.4—Marriage lines

what factors separate an "emotionally important" love relationship from one that is less important isn't clear.

In *Palmistry for All* (1916) the eminent hand reader Cheiro wrote, "Only the clearly formed lines relate to marriage, the short ones to deep affection, or marriage contemplated but never entered into" (73). Cheiro (a rather interesting chap whose real name was either Count Louis Hamon or William John Warner) then goes into intensive detail concerning various qualities of the marriage lines and what they predict.

In an earlier book, *Language of the Hand* (1897), Cheiro goes into even more detail about numerous "Lines of Influence" that can affect the marriage lines. However, Cheiro was a wise and practical man well acquainted with human nature, and he knew that not all marriages are love-matches. Even during his time in England in the sexually repressed Victorian era, illicit affairs and dalliances were the rule rather than the exception. Cheiro always began his discussions with little verses of his own devising, and about the lines of marriage he wrote:

What matter if the words be said,
The license paid—they are not wed;
Unless love link each heart to heart,
'Twere better keep these lives apart.

In other words, bad judgment should not be mistaken for true love.

Most palmists find that reading the marriage lines is a lot like predicting the weather: sometimes they are right on, sometimes they are not even in the ball-park. People will have marriage lines over brief affairs, and I've seen people who were married several times with only one marriage line, or none. A friend of mine told me about a possessive mother who developed a marriage line over her adult son who lived at home with her. Furthermore, what can the marriage lines indicate in polygamous societies, where a person may have several spouses simultaneously?

Indian palmist S. K. Das (*Everybody's Guide to Palmistry*, 1986) tells us that "the Line of Marriage is also called the line of union or attachment or liaison . . . It does not necessarily show marriage; it may only indicate attachment to some-one, male or female" (171). In other words, this line can indicate anyone whom you consider a friend or loved one. He goes on to say that this line is often found on spinsters, celibates, and eunuchs (I must admit that I've never done a reading for a eunuch!), and in such cases indicates strong friendship. J. S. Bright, in *The Dictionary of Palmistry* (1958), calls them "Affection Lines" and comments, "Every Affection Line . . . does not necessarily represent marriage but it does rep-resent an affection that you have felt or will feel for someone" (118).

In other words, you either currently have a friend, had a friend at some time in the past, or will have a friend someday! Hmm, talk about covering all the bases—no wonder many palmists avoid trying to read these ambiguous lines at all!

In my opinion, this type of generalization of the marriage line trivializes its sig-nificance and waters down any practical usefulness it may have. It is obvious that marriage lines do not actually indicate how many times a person will be married. On the other hand, it doesn't make sense that a signpost as important as this could be dependent on ephemeral social factors such as changing sexual mores and the local definition of marriage. That these lines are connected with relationships is an observation that goes back hundreds of years, and it's a valid one, as we will see. The problem of interpretation is caused by a simple fact: marriage is a social convention, not a spiritual or karmic one. So as social conventions change, so will the interpretation of the marriage line.

Times change; karma, however, does not.

The confusion surrounding marriage lines disappears when we understand that they do not indicate marital partners, but soul mates; that is, members of our soul family. Marriage lines indicate relationships with members of our soul families who are in flesh. Because these lines indicate a karmic relationship, I prefer to call them *lines of karmic attachment* (or *lines of attachment* for short). For example, if you have three lines of attachment, this predicts you will meet three of your soul mates and have satisfying, educational relationships with each of them.

SOUL MATES

It comes as a surprise to most people to learn that they can have more than one soul mate. A popular romantic notion is that a soul mate is someone with whom you are locked in a romantic relationship forever and always. As romantic as this notion may be, what could we possibly learn from being with the same person forever? Since the role of a soul mate is to help us work on specific lessons, it isn't surprising to find that as our lessons change, so do our soul mates.

In his excellent book *Soul Mates*, Richard Webster describes a man who married three of his soul mates one after another. Each relationship was a coming together of kindred spirits and each taught the man a valuable lesson, which helped him pay his karmic debt and progress spiritually. Soul mates come together, learn from each other, and move apart, time and time again, lifetime after lifetime.

TYPES OF RELATIONSHIPS

The quality of the line of attachment suggests the importance and intensity of the relationship. A long, thick line represents a relationship that lasts for years and culminates in valuable, soul-maturing lessons. Shorter lines usually indicate briefer, but no less important, relationships that teach us hard lessons about ourselves.

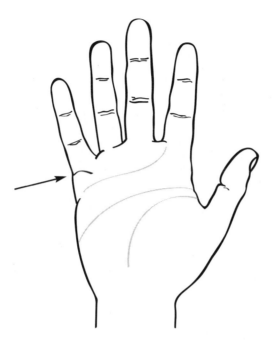

Figure 6.5—A downward-curving marriage line

When the line curves downward toward the heart line (Figure 6.5), it means that you will enjoy a close, loving relationship, but you will probably outlive that particular soul mate. If you've ever had a dear friend, lover, or teacher who passed away after helping you on the road to spiritual maturity, then you are familiar with this experience. Once the lesson is over and you have the tools you need to complete the work, the teacher returns to the spiritual plane. You have to finish the work by yourself. It's time to fly solo.

When the line curves upward toward the little finger (Figure 6.6), the relationship will probably entail arguing and conflicts of will. The lessons are revealed through debate and sparring. Have you ever seen a married couple who constantly argues but can't seem to stay apart from each other for any length of time; or friends who criticize each other's actions and decisions; or families who seem to be one step away from killing each other but flock together during times of crisis? If so, you are probably familiar with this concept.

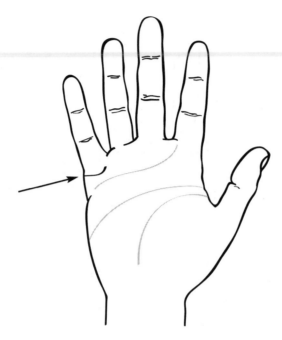

Figure 6.6—An upward-curving marriage line

HOW MANY LINES?

Notice that many people have several lines of karmic attachment, while others have only one or none. Those with one line will probably meet and marry their soul mate and enjoy a close relationship until one or both of them pass away. Those with several lines will enjoy many teachers throughout life, and travel quite far on their spiritual journey. The odds are very good that they will marry one or more of their soul mates and have a happy marriage.

Those with no lines of attachment should not worry, though. They could still meet their soul mate(s). The lack of attachment lines does not mean that someone will be alone all his or her life. These lines appear and disappear as we age. Sometimes a lack of lines of attachment means that part of our lesson is that the meetings of soul family will come out of the blue when we least expect it. In other words, it's one of those things we're just not meant to know.

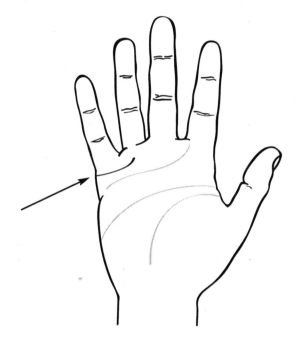

Figure 6.7—A long attachment line

NOT ALL ROADS ARE SMOOTH

Of course, all relationships, karmic or otherwise, have complications. We can predict the nature of these complications through certain signs.

A long attachment line, one that stretches past the confines of the area beneath the little finger (Figure 6.7), denotes a relationship with a lover that spans many lifetimes. This is the common perception of the term *soul mate*. The longer the line, the further back the two of you go.

A three-pronged fork on an attachment line (Figure 6.8) indicates a blessing, but of a mixed kind. It indicates that the person may be blessed with one lover too many! He or she must learn the pitfalls of the ménage à trois, for the middle line represents an intruding lover that must be dealt with. My grandmother used to call this configuration the "fickle fork," which refers to the difficulties the person sporting one may have staying faithful.

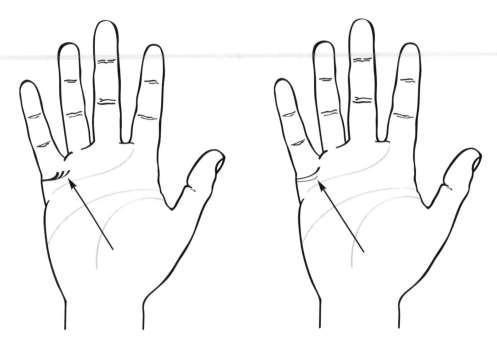

Figures 6.8 and 6.9—Three-pronged fork on the attachment line (left)
and almost parallel lines of attachment (right)

Two lines of attachment that run almost parallel (Figure 6.9) indicate a businesslike relationship. The couple may stay together for years, but live emotionally separate lives. These relationships usually end after a specific task is completed. Often, they will go their separate ways after the children are raised, for example. Usually, the separated partners will remain close friends.

A fine parallel line is called a companion line (Figure 6.10). It indicates a person who cannot find complete satisfaction in a marriage. He or she will need something else—a job, a beloved hobby, or, in some cases, an affair—to feel complete.

KARMIC ADVERSARIES

Lines that travel vertically from the heel of the hand toward the pad of the thumb are called *lines of adversity* or *opposition* (Figure 6.11). They indicate periods where we learn through conflict. Some Eastern schools of palmistry say these

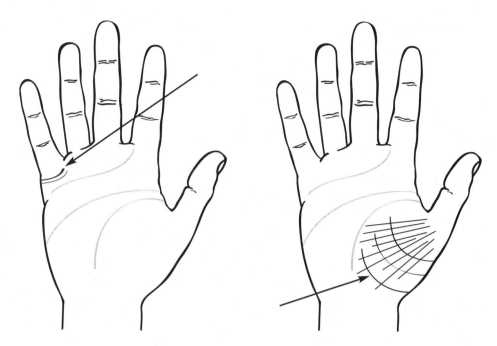

Figures 6.10 and 6.11—A companion line (left) and lines of opposition (right)

lines indicate the number of enemies we attract to ourselves. However, these opponents are here to help us, oddly enough. I call such an opponent a "karmic adversary"; someone who brings out the best in us through the dynamics of battle. This can be a business or romantic rival; a competitor in our chosen field; or a younger, more aggressive version of us. Being humans, we learn through struggle, and sometimes we need the competition of an opponent to force us to grow.

In *The Teachings of Don Juan* by Carlos Castaneda, the apprentice sorcerer discovers that he is the object of magickal assault from another, more powerful sorcerer. In order to defend himself and survive the attacks, Castaneda must learn to be a more powerful sorcerer. Rarely are karmic adversaries life-threatening, but they do keep you on your toes.

Sometimes the line of adversity indicates a situation that forces us to re-evaluate our direction, such as a dead-end job. At any rate, forward progress is retarded until we learn the necessary skills to escape the adversarial situation. These lines are directly related to our behavior in the previous life, and indicate periods where we're vigorously working off our karmic debt. In other words, ouch!

CHILDREN LINES

The children lines (Figure 6.12) are another source of trouble for hand readers. Traditionally, the lines are supposed to indicate the number of children the person will have. However, as with marriage lines, the children lines are sometimes right on and sometimes not even close. They appear to have been rendered obsolete with the passage of time and the greater degree of control we have on our procreation. With birth control, fertility treatments, and adoption, a person has almost total control over the number of children he or she will parent.

However, just like marriage lines, I couldn't believe that such an important feature of the hand could be invalidated by the invention of birth control technology. Therefore I've come to the conclusion that the children lines represent the number of children a person must have in his or her life in order to fulfill the emotional need of parenting. As such, the children lines represent soul family members who are waiting to appear in your life as children. These soul mates can appear as children whom you physically parent, adopted children, stepchildren, or sometimes even pets, as animals seem to be part of our soul families too. These "spiritual children" are waiting for us when we're ready to open our life and heart to them. Have you ever heard the phrase "He was like a father to me," or "She was like a mother to me"? Obviously, this is a karmic parent/child relationship; two members of the same soul family coming together.

Not too long ago I did a reading for a young woman in her twenties who had been diagnosed with cervical cancer. Her prognosis was good, but the doctor warned her that the condition might make it impossible for her to have children. This was a major source of concern because she dreamed of having a big family someday. Since she had three children lines on her hand, I was able to tell her that there were three children waiting for her. Whether she physically gave birth to these three soul mates or not, they were her children, for she was destined from birth to be their parent. "Whether you actually give birth to them," I told her, "or adopt, or have stepchildren, or maybe a little animal that you take into your heart and your home, these are *your* children, all three of them. They are there for you, and nothing can take them

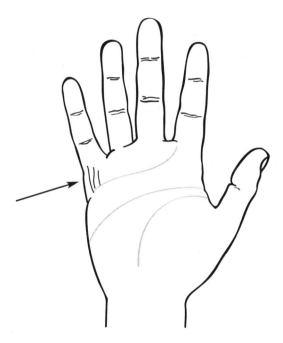

Figure 6.12—Children lines

away from you." Needless to say, this was a great comfort to her. The karmic lesson from the cervical cancer was for her to learn to expand her definition of the parent/child relationship.

With this karmic interpretation of the children lines we see that they can be incredibly accurate. So pervasive is this karmic parenting that often we see people practice it without knowing it. One of my clients, who has three very well-defined children lines, has no biological children of her own. However, during the course of our discussions it became apparent that she had been "practicing" parenthood for several years. At her current job, she had taken three of the younger employees under her wing and helped them not only with their job duties, but with personal problems as well. When I pointed this out to her, she recalled her previous job as a restaurant manager where she had "adopted" two waitresses and one waiter and helped them deal with personal problems. She thought further back, all the way to her childhood, and saw this pattern of mothering three children repeating itself over and over. "I even had three Barbie dolls!" she told me. This is just one of countless examples of how karma nudges us into fulfilling our potential.

Sometimes we'll see people who have more children in their life than children lines on their hand. They've taken on more than their share of karmic responsibility.

Further evidence that karmic children find their parents can be observed in a fairly common phenomenon: have you ever noticed how often adopted children resemble one of the parents? Earlier I mentioned that karmic children sometimes manifest themselves as pets. A lot of people think I'm kidding when I say this, but just as adopted children sometimes resemble their parents, have you ever noticed the same resemblance between certain pets and their owners? Karma finds a way to bring us together with our soul mates, no matter what the obstacles.

Very small, hard-to-see children lines can sometimes indicate that the person has had a miscarriage or otherwise terminated pregnancy, whether she knows it or not. Sad as this situation seems to us, we must realize that it, too, serves karma. Sometimes when a person dies an unnatural death—as in an accident or murder—his or her soul prefers to come back and be reborn just long enough to die a more natural death.

> *By persistence are great empires built.*
> *There is no law beyond do what thou wilt,*
> *Lust of result mars will in every way;*
> *But steadfast purpose spans the vast abysm.*
>
> —I Ching

chapter seven

PALMISTRY, CHAKRAS, & HAND REFLEXOLOGY

*Happiness is when what you think, what you
say, and what you do are in harmony.*

—Mahatma Gandhi, *Gandhi:
An Autobiography*

Chakras are invisible portals that lie within the human electromagnetic field (or aura, if you prefer). Through the chakras, various energies—including the life force itself—are received and transmitted to different locations in the body. The word *chakra* is Sanskrit for "wheel," and is used because these portals are perceived as spinning circular vortexes. The chakras regulate the flow of vital energies into and from the body, and, many believe, must be properly maintained and exercised to facilitate health, happiness, and spiritual growth. These chakras will be familiar to practitioners of kundalini yoga.

Since we accept that everything we experience is reflected in the hand, it stands to reason that there must be palmistry regions that represent the chakras. Figure 7.1 shows the locations of the chakras as they are commonly represented.

Figure 7.1—The chakras

Figure 7.2 shows the reflex points of the seven chakras in the hand. We will examine these areas in more detail as we work on balancing our chakras.

NUMBER ONE: THE ROOT CHAKRA

The root chakra, or kundalini, is the first chakra, and it is located at the base of the spine. It is represented by the color red, which symbolizes passion, drive, determination, anger, survival, all physical sensations (including pain and pleasure), and will power. The root chakra connects us to the earth, and is responsible for our physical grounding. Therefore, it is the first and most important chakra to balance, since we must have a firm grounding before we develop the other, higher chakras.

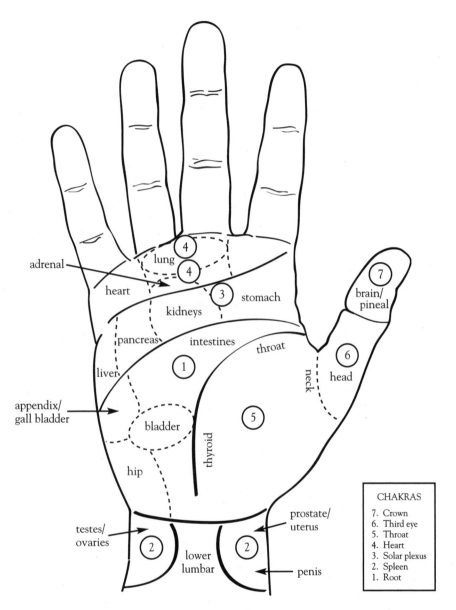

Figure 7.2—*The reflex points of the chakras in the hand*

In the figure, the following labels appear:

- adrenal
- lung — 4
- 4
- heart
- 3 — stomach
- kidneys
- 7 — brain/ pineal
- pancreas
- intestines
- throat
- 6
- neck — head
- liver
- 1
- appendix/ gall bladder
- bladder
- 5
- thyroid
- hip
- prostate/ uterus
- testes/ ovaries
- 2 — lower lumbar — 2
- penis

CHAKRAS

7. Crown
6. Third eye
5. Throat
4. Heart
3. Solar plexus
2. Spleen
1. Root

The symptoms of an overactive root chakra are greed, obesity, uncontrolled anger, and sluggishness. An underactive root chakra can lead to anxiety, restlessness, anorexia, and problems with concentration. Physical symptoms can include problems with the lower body (such as poor circulation in the feet and legs), constipation, addictive behavior, and problems sleeping due to anxiety.

Balancing the root chakra is easy. Dancing, physical exercise, and a walk in the woods are all therapeutic. Also, simply taking care of the mundane details of daily existence—housework, dishes, laundry—helps balance the root energies. I find that organizing my work area helps me feel better grounded.

In terms of palmistry, I often help balance the root chakra by rolling clay between my palms, which stimulates its reflex point. A friend of mine prefers to work in her garden when she feels the need to connect with her earthy energies. Digging with the trowel firmly stimulates the root chakra's reflex point in the palm of the hand.

We can also use the reflex points identified in Figure 7.2, area 1 (the area defined between the head line and the life line) to help accelerate the balancing process. Massage the area firmly several times a day while concentrating on balancing the root energies.

It is important to have a healthy, well-balanced root chakra, as it is responsible for manifesting potential into reality. It can give us unlimited energy, optimism, and the capacity to examine and develop all our other chakras. It is the source from which everything else arises, so tend it well!

NUMBER TWO: THE SPLEEN CHAKRA

Related to the water element and the color orange, the second chakra is connected to emotions, sexual relationships, and the ability to accept change. Its Sanskrit name is *svadhisthana,* which means "sweetness." This energy center is located directly below the navel.

If the spleen chakra is overactive, it can lead to overindulgence, lack of emotional control, manipulation of others, and self-delusion. When underactive, it can lead to clinginess, dependency on others, shyness, feelings of guilt, frigidity, impotence, or loss of interest in favorite activities. Some of the physical manifestations include kidney or bladder problems, lack of energy, and allergies.

Often, the spleen chakra is out of kilter due to emotional repression during childhood. People who grew up in repressed, stern, or critical environments may need quite a bit of work to unblock the spleen energies. The areas of Figure 7.2 marked with the number 2 show the reflex points located on either side of the wrist that correspond to the spleen chakra. Other techniques for balancing the spleen are hula dancing (I'm serious—moving the hips helps a lot!); engaging in creative, childlike forms of self-expression such as fingerpainting, drawing, or working with clay; laughing; and generally acting silly. Sometimes collecting favorite toys from childhood, or collecting toys you would have loved to have but didn't, helps release clogged spleen energy.

From a palmistry/hand reflexology point of view, gentle massage of the areas of the wrist designated by the number 2 in Figure 7.2 can help balance the spleen chakra. These areas are very sensitive and, in most people, are erogenous zones.

We find as we unblock and balance the spleen chakra we become more compassionate, exhibit a greater concern for others, and enjoy an effortless freedom of expression. We also find our romantic and sexual relationships deeper and more satisfying.

NUMBER THREE: THE SOLAR PLEXUS CHAKRA

Located just below the breastbone, the solar plexus chakra, also known by its Sanskrit name *manipura*, is our control center. It affects personal power, metabolism, sense of identity, and finding our place in the universe. It is represented by the color yellow, which symbolizes the fire element. In martial arts, the solar plexus is the center of chi energy.

A well-balanced third chakra gives us a cheerful, outgoing confidence and a strong sense of self-respect. Consequently, we treat others with greater consideration. We become skillful in our craft, intelligent, spontaneous, and eager to take on new challenges. We learn to enjoy the delicious fruits of being alive: good food, good friends, and physical activities.

An underactive third chakra can make us feel depressed, uninterested, and insecure. Sometimes it can cause poor digestion, food allergies, liver problems, breathing problems, gallstones, and abdominal cramps. An overactive third chakra can cause us to become obsessed with work, critical and perfectionistic, unreasonable, possessive, and emotionally inhibited.

The most effective way to balance the solar plexus chakra is through yogic breathing exercises. Sit in a relaxed lotus position with your legs crossed and elbows resting on your knees, or comfortably in a straight-backed chair. Take deep, slow breaths, making sure you use the muscles of your diaphragm to draw each breath. Diaphragmatic breathing is deeper than upper-chest breathing, and it enriches the body with oxygen. Alternate these breathing exercises with a firm massage of the area indicated in Figure 7.2, reflex point number 3, located between the head and heart lines. Pay particular attention to the nerve center under the second finger.

NUMBER FOUR: THE HEART CHAKRA

The heart chakra concerns itself with—what else?—love. It is represented by the color green, and its Sanskrit name is *anahata*, which, interestingly enough, means "unstruck." The fourth chakra's element is air, which warns us that accepting reality, rather than giving in to romantic illusions, will be a challenge. An overactive heart chakra can make a person demanding, jealous, possessive, melodramatic, and moody. Often people with an overactive heart chakra are masters of manipulative behavior, using sex and love as tools for controlling others. An underactive heart chakra can lead to feelings of unworthiness ("No one will *ever* love someone like me!"), paranoia, and self-pity. Since we crave most what we don't have, people with weak heart chakras want desperately to be loved. Most of our fear of rejection stems from a blocked heart chakra. Some of the health problems related to the fourth chakra are heart problems, high blood pressure, fatigue, some asthmas, insomnia, and a weakening of the immune system.

Working from our palmistry point of view tells us that massaging area number 4 of Figure 7.2—the mounts found just beneath the fingers—can help open and balance the heart chakra. However, reflexology alone will not solve everything. We must learn to take risks, to open our heart to others no matter how scary that may seem, and practice the art of romance. Go with a loved one to romantic movies, take lessons in ballroom dancing, and learn to give to others without thought of payback. Be more physical in your affections—hug and touch others more (respectfully, of course). Don't be afraid of being sappy. It's a heck of a lot better than being cynical!

The heart chakra is the portal through which we absorb the emotional energy of others. This is an area of great vulnerability and must be well protected. I've learned that empathic persons are frequently overwhelmed by other people's negative emotional energy. They, and everyone for that matter, can certainly benefit from learning to close the heart chakra at will. An easy exercise for doing this is to simply turn the backs of the hands toward the person from whom the negativity is emanating. We do this automatically when we cross our arms in a defensive posture, but this bit of body language can tell the other person that we're closing him or her off. Turning the backs of the hands toward the source of the disturbance is just as effective, and it doesn't offend anybody in the process.

NUMBER FIVE: THE THROAT CHAKRA

This is the chakra associated with communication. Its Sanskrit name is *visshudha*, which means "purification," and it is represented by a pure sky-blue. The throat chakra's element is sound.

An overactive throat chakra is easy to identify. The person can't seem to get the words out fast enough. Often there is stuttering, frequent interrupting of others, and an inability to stop talking long enough to listen. An underdeveloped throat chakra, however, causes the person to be terrified of speaking. Often the person's speech is marked by long pauses and difficulty finding the right words.

The throat chakra is sensitive to deception; often when telling a falsehood or speaking insincerely, we'll choke up. The same thing happens when we're forced to repress something we strongly need to say; it feels like a particle of food caught in the throat. Some of the physical effects of a weak throat chakra include sore throat, laryngitis, thyroid problems, and stuttering.

Someone with a well-balanced throat chakra has a pleasant, mellifluous voice; knows when to speak and when to listen; and is good at self-expression. They tend to speak honestly and directly.

Notice in Figure 7.2 the area associated with the throat chakra (number 5) comprises the whole Mount of Venus. This shows the relationship between passion and speech, and the voice and vitality. The spoken word is magick; it can create or destroy. A powerful voice bespeaks a strong, charismatic person. Balancing the throat chakra is accomplished through humming, singing, and controlling the breath as you talk. My favorite technique is reading poetry out loud. Humming the sound "mmmmm" repeatedly and letting the syllable resonate through the sinuses and head is a great throat-chakra opener.

A very useful hand exercise for balancing the throat chakra involves rubbing the Mounts of Venus (the pads of the hands) together. Notice that you do this automatically when you're about to give a speech, or when confronted with the task of delivering bad news. Stimulation of the Mounts of Venus boosts the power of the throat chakra, and is a handy trick to remember during those times when speech becomes difficult.

NUMBER SIX: THE THIRD-EYE CHAKRA

The third-eye, or brow, chakra, is associated with the act of seeing clearly—both intuitively and with the eyes. Its element is the energy of consciousness. The Sanskrit name is *ajna,* which means "to perceive," and it is represented by the color indigo. Located in the middle of the forehead between the eyebrows, the third-eye chakra is the center of all psychic powers. Through the sixth chakra we receive vision, guidance, and higher intuition. This is the portal through which we invite past lives, telepathy, and spirit visions.

When hyperactive, the third-eye chakra can make a person egocentric and vain. These people tend to mistake the ego's agenda for the calling of the Higher Self, and often try to dominate others through religious or spiritual dogma. When underactive, the person can become listless, oversensitive to the opinions of others, and afraid of success.

When the third-eye chakra is well balanced, however, life's richest experiences await. The person with a well-balanced third-eye chakra is unattached to the material world, unaffected by the opinions and actions of others, and sees clearly the difference between what is important in life and what is a waste of time. This is the tool for developing clairvoyance, clairaudience, and the ability to channel.

To balance the sixth chakra, meditate in a prone position with a clear crystal on your forehead, chant the sacred syllable "Om" as you practice yogic breathing, and visualize the color indigo. Alternate these meditation sessions with a firm massage of the middle joint of the thumb (the area marked with a "6" in Figure 7.2). This combination of palmistry/reflexology and meditation can really bring fast results.

NUMBER SEVEN: THE CROWN CHAKRA

Lastly, we come to the most beautiful and highest point of all: the crown chakra. Represented by a lovely violet hue and located at the top of the head, it is related to the highest spiritual state possible to attain. Its element is light. Its Sanskrit name, *sahasrara*, means "thousandfold" and refers to the infinite nature of developed spiritual awareness. This is the realm of pure spirit; where awareness is perfect, complete, and all-encompassing.

Notice that in Figure 7.2, the crown chakra is linked to the tip of the thumb (area number 7), which represents will power. This is important to remember as we study the link between the hand and the chakras. Massaging this area stimulates the pineal gland, which is said to be important in the development of the seventh chakra.

Yet even this wonderful jewel can be overstimulated. When hyperactive, the crown energies can cause a person to become overly intellectual and to lose contact with the material world. There is a constant state of frustration caused by the impossibility of taking the spiritual purity so strongly sensed somewhere "out there" and manifesting it in the "real" world. Manic depression and destructive tendencies can follow. Not all spiritual visions are creative and positive; one has only to look at the Nazis' obsession with the occult to realize this.

When underdeveloped, however, the deficiency of crown energy can lead to skepticism toward all things spiritual, a lack of joy, and a rather mundane, materialistic view of the world. For such people, psychic phenomena and spiritual experiences simply do not exist.

Ah, but when balanced and controlled, the crown energy can be used to heal, to transcend the laws of nature, and to work magick. To balance the seventh chakra is to know the Mind of God. This is why the crown chakra is often depicted as a halo; the saints of old called upon the Higher Power to work miracles.

To balance and develop the crown chakra, we must first create a state of perfect balance in the lower six chakras. Once we've accomplished this—and it can take a lifetime—we become a clear, perfect circuit for the Higher Power. The chakras complete the circuit—the root chakra connecting us to the earth and the crown chakra connecting us to heaven. Once we've created this perfect state of spiritual equilibrium, we become Illuminated; a creature of pure light, freed from the karmic cycle of death and rebirth, worthy of claiming our spiritual birthright as a tiny fragment of the Universal Mind.

> *One glad morning*
> *When this life is over*
> *I'll fly away . . .*
>
> —Traditional American spiritual

chapter eight
THE KARMIC ELEMENTS

> *The comparison of the right hand with the*
> *left hand shows the true inner task or mission*
> *of a person.*
>
> —Julius Spiers, *The Hands of Children*

*A*s I mentioned in *Runic Palmistry*, I have a great fondness for the method of classifying hands into the elements earth, air, fire, and water. According to Terrence Dukes in his excellent (if difficult to grasp) book *Chinese Hand Analysis*, these elements are used in the Wu Hsing method of hand reading as practiced within the Chen Yen Esoteric Buddhism tradition. Thus, it fits right in with our discussion of karma. In addition to the four classical elements, we'll learn about two other important elements from traditional Chinese hand reading: wood and metal. In fact, in traditional Chinese divination, the five elements are earth, water, wood, metal, and fire—no air. Air seems to have drifted in from Western influences. We'll examine this element later.

In this chapter we'll learn how to determine what element your hand falls into, the characteristics of each element, and the karmic implications of each hand type.

Typing a hand is not as simple as it seems at first glance. Although there are only six elemental types, many people do not fall neatly into any one elemental category. Typically, you'll find that the fingers are of one type and the palm of another. The person will be a blend of the two hand types. Adding to this complexity is that some people's left and right hands will exhibit different elements. Just keep in mind that the dominant hand shows the person's social element—that is, who the person is at the present time, based on the external pressures of society. To read the person's karmic element, or the element given at birth, we look at the passive hand.

It is possible, even with hands with two or more elements, to reduce the hand to a single element by determining which type the subject's hand resembles most, and eliminating weaker elements. The rule to remember is: wood conquers earth, earth conquers water, water conquers fire, fire conquers metal, and metal conquers wood (think of an ax felling a tree). Therefore, if a hand is a fire/water mixture, we can safely call it a water hand, since water conquers fire. An earth/water mixture is an earth type, since earth conquers water.

You probably noticed that the air element is missing from the rule. As we said earlier, air is a relatively modern addition to the elements of the hand. It is most likely an influence of Western tradition and comes from the ancient Greeks, although it may be related to the element ether from Hindu palmistry. Air can be said to conquer everything; after all, nothing can live without air. Air combines with metal to cause rust, and what can withstand the force of a hurricane? Lack of air is a vacuum; that is to say, nothingness. Without air, human life is impossible, so perhaps it's the most important element of all.

MEASURING THE FINGER/PALM RATIO

The first technique we'll learn is to determine if the hand has a square or rectangular palm. A square palm is close to the same length at its widest point as it is at its broadest point (Figure 8.1). If the palm is noticeably longer in either direction, it is rectangular. You can use a ruler or calipers to determine this ratio if you like.

It's a little trickier to determine finger length. Some people have a knack for determining finger length through visual inspection only. If this is a problem for

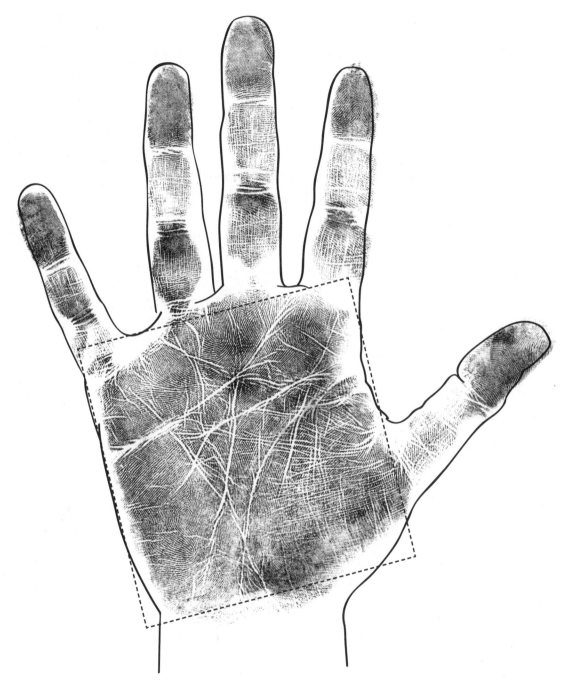

Figure 8.1—A square palm with long fingers

you (and it is, sometimes, for me), there are many ways to do this other than by visual inspection. Again, you can use a ruler or calipers. Long fingers are almost as long as the palm is wide, and short fingers fall shorter than the palm's width. Obviously, the hand print shown in Figure 8.1 has long fingers, while Figure 8.2 shows the hand of a person with short fingers.

I recall my early days doing psychic fairs when I carried a little toolcase containing a ruler, an angle measurer (an orthopedic instrument to measure the angle of the thumb), a set of calipers, and an illuminated magnifying glass. I still use some of these tools today if I run into a hand that I have trouble classifying.

The most practical method for determining finger length is one suggested by Fred Gettings in *The Book of the Hand*. Fred Gettings wrote several very valuable books for the serious palmist, and I highly recommend them to you for further study. To use the Gettings method for determining finger length, you'll need a compass (such as used in drafting to draw circles), ink, paper, and a hand to measure, of course.

First, make a print of the hand. If you're working in a venue where you don't have time to make prints, such as a psychic fair or house party, there's another method I'll describe shortly. For now, let's assume that we have all the time in the world, and no place in particular we have to be. Place the point of the compass on the point at the base of the second finger (Saturn), and adjust it so that the radius is the tip of the second finger.

Now, using the base of the Saturn finger as the center, draw a complete circle (Figure 8.3). If the circle encompasses most of the hand, including the thumb, the fingers are long. If the circle falls well within the area of the palm and misses the tip of the thumb, the fingers are short (Figure 8.4). Obviously, there will be a lot of variation from hand to hand, but this method is extremely reliable.

If you're not working from a print, you can use my "finger compass" method. Place the tip of your thumb at the base of Saturn and the tip of your forefinger at the tip of Saturn. Keeping your thumb firmly in place and using the forefinger as a compass, swing your forefinger around in a circle, taking care not to alter the distance between it and your thumb. Mentally visualize the circle and make your determinations as in the Gettings method. With practice, this method works almost as well as working from a print with a real compass.

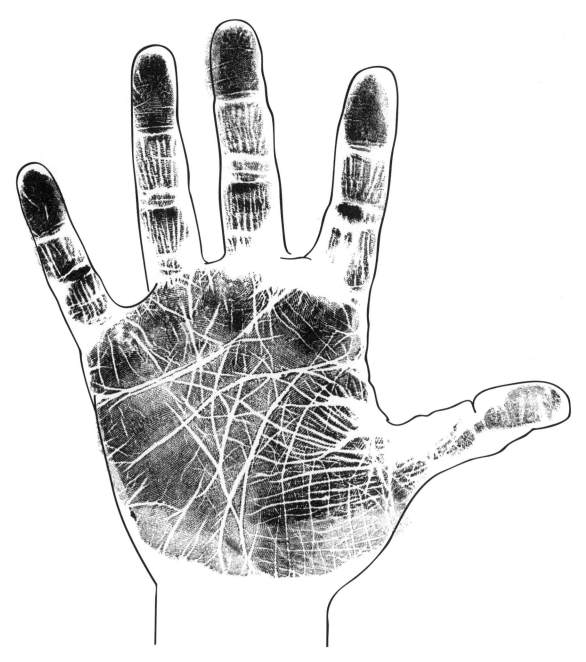

Figure 8.2—A square palm with short fingers

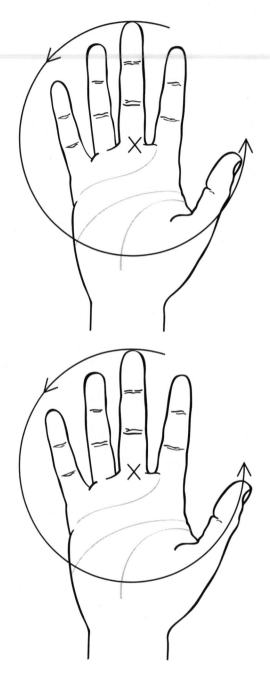

Figures 8.3 and 8.4—A hand with long fingers (top) and a hand with short fingers (bottom)

So now we know how to determine whether the palm is square or rectangular, and if the fingers are long or short. Now let's see what we can do with this information.

THE EARTH HAND

The earth hand (Figure 8.5) is usually the easiest of the four types to recognize. The qualities to look for are a square, fleshy palm, short fingers, and very few lines. The few lines reflect a preference for simplicity. If the fingers are rounded at the tips, the person may be a bit impatient. Square tips suggest a person who thinks a little bit more before acting. You have to be careful not to mistake this hand type for the metal hand, which has a square palm, square fingers, and is harder to the touch than the earth hand. The earth hand is similar to the "Practical Hand" of classical palmistry.

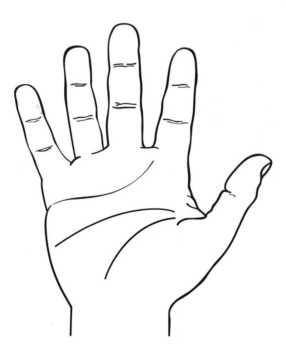

Figure 8.5—The earth hand

The subject possessing an earth hand will be practical, down-to-earth (naturally), reliable, predictable, emotionally stable, and often conservative. The line patterns of these hands are usually very simple, which reflects the person's simple and direct approach to life.

Earth hands denote people who are fond of tradition. Their motto is "If it isn't broke, don't fix it." They possess a strong work ethic, are punctual, and tend to provide for the future. They neither lead nor follow, instead preferring to do things their own way in their own time.

Think of the earth when you see this hand. Mountains and trees tend to be very stable and move slowly. The earth is fertile, so this hand reveals an active interest in sex. Although earth types usually aren't the most passionate romantics, they are nurturing and supportive. For the person with an earth hand, relationships do not burn like fire, nor do they flow like water, but are sources of security and stability.

Earth types should look for their soul mates among other earths, wood types, and, sometimes, among the more stable water types. They do not do well with fire types, as the emotional intensity can scorch them. Also, earths seem a bit boring to the intense fire type.

The karmic challenge for earth types is to learn to open themselves to new experiences. Sometimes the walls of security can become a prison. "If you don't try it, how do you know you don't like it?"

Career: Architect, craftsperson, merchant, accountant, and designer. Earth types are usually fond of plants and animals.

THE FIRE HAND

Fire hands (Figure 8.6) have short fingers, which denotes impatience, and a long palm, which indicates vast reserves of emotional energy. The fire hand is usually hot to the touch. People with this hand type are passionate and intense. They love change and variety, and become easily bored with tedious work. They hate restrictions, limitations, or falling into a rut.

People with fire hands possess strong desires, appetites, and ambition. They are great starters, but they seldom finish their projects, especially if the work takes too long. They become inflamed with an idea, but lack the patience to see it

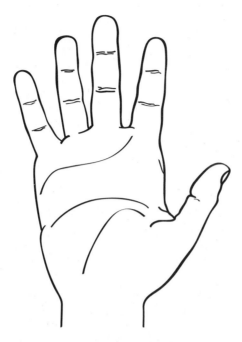

Figure 8.6—The fire hand

through. For example, they will often start novels, screenplays, or home improve-ments, but often leave them unfinished. They become bored if something takes too long to finish, and rush off to begin a new project! Fire types and earth types work well together; the fire person starts the project and turns it over to the earth, who finishes it.

Fire types are ambitious, and if the fire element is too strong, it can make the person greedy and power-hungry. A fire hand with a tempering element of earth is ideal. Fire types have to be reminded how their actions affect others. Otherwise their ambition can cause them to run over other people on their way to their goal.

Fire can only burn so long. Addicted to intense action, fire types will frequently crash after a period of strenuous activity. They can accomplish a great deal in a short amount of time though.

Fire types should seek their soul mates among other fire types who share simi-lar goals, or among the imaginative air types, whom they see as a constant source of stimulation. Water isn't a fortunate element for fire types, as water smothers fire. Earth tends to be a bit too stable to hold a fire's attention for long.

The karmic challenge for fire types is to learn to use power and leadership qualities wisely. Probably in a past life they were guilty of misusing power and must learn to control it in this life.

Career: Massage therapist, military, law enforcement, explorer, model, surgeon, income tax consultant, paramedic.

THE AIR HAND

Recognizable by its square palm and long fingers, the air hand (Figure 8.7) denotes a person with a quick, agile mind. The negative side of air types is their tendency to deceive and manipulate. Air types are great self-motivators and work according to their own inner agenda. They can be a bit flamboyant in their behavior, and sometimes will act in a contrived manner to elicit a desired response from others. Consequently, they don't always mean what they say.

As natural entertainers, air types tend to enjoy attention and recognition. They thrive on mental challenges and work well under a deadline. Sometimes they seem to be addicted to stress and melodrama. Naturally explorative and curious, an air type will try anything at least once.

Air types are versatile and multisided; it is as though they have several different people living in their head. Many actors and actresses sport an air hand. Airs are great at debate and often will argue either side of an issue just for the fun of it. They enjoy psychology and playing mind games with themselves as well as others. People with this hand are very good at generating concepts, theories, and ideas (sowing the seeds), although they seldom find the time to act on all of them.

The karmic challenge for air types is multifold. They must learn to work with others, to take their idealism and make it practical, and to get out of their head and into the real world.

Air types should find their soul mates among other airs or among fire types, as long as they take care to not let the fire type burn them out. Air types sometimes feel restricted and limited in a relationship with the more conventional earth type.

Career: Lawyer, entertainer, teacher, linguist, author, magician, naturalist, pilot, driver, computer worker, archaeologist, draftsperson, musician.

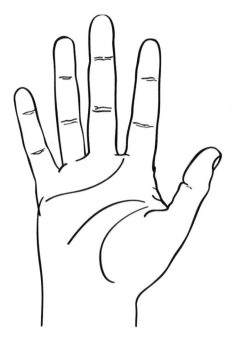

Figure 8.7—The air hand

THE WATER HAND

A water hand (Figure 8.8) has a rectangular palm, is very soft and flexible, and has many fine lines and long, smoothly tapered fingers. Water is the most volatile and unstable of the four elements. Earth is always earth, and fire is always fire, but water can be liquid, solid, or gaseous. It can be said that water can assume the state of the other three elements as well as its own. Therefore water types tend to be moody, and at times their external appearance is completely at odds with the internal reality. "You can't judge a book by its cover" is definitely true of water types. They are often plagued by mood swings and conflicting impulses as they shift from an earthlike (solid) state to an airlike (gaseous) state. Also, the long fingers denote perfectionism and a sensitivity to detail. Water types can be difficult to please.

Because of the myriad tiny lines covering the surface, water hands tend to look old. However, the lines have nothing to do with age, but with the intensity of their emotional expression.

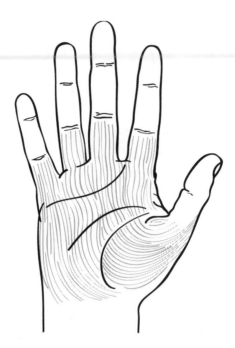

Figure 8.8—The water hand

It's difficult to read water types' moods from their face as "still waters run deep." They are watchers and observers. This holds especially true if the fingers are knobby. Water types love to watch and observe others.

Water types are restless, and need a grounding influence or they will tend to scatter their energy all over the place. They approach subjects indirectly and can talk for hours about nothing in particular. However, when grounded by a solid relationship, religious doctrine, or profession, they can be tremendously productive and creative. Because they love to approach a subject from oblique angles, water types have unique perspectives and their own way of doing things.

Sometimes water types tend to be sensitive to criticism and often see rejection where none was intended. On the other hand, they can be quite intuitive, and their first impressions of people are often right on target.

Water types should seek their soul mates among other water types, wood types, or among the less-restricted members of the earth type (the secure boundaries of earth helps contain the restless water element). Water and fire can work together in business with powerful results (and sex between a fire and water type can be "steamy!"), but for a long-term relationship, the mixture is too volatile. The fire type will eventually feel smothered by the water element.

The karmic challenge for water types is to find a suitable channel for their flowing energy. They must direct the wellsprings of their talents into a useful and productive endeavor. This sometimes takes quite a bit of experimentation.

Career: Poet; science fiction, horror, and fantasy writer; nurse; social worker; personnel manager; public relations; advertising; musician; working with children; religious work; sailor; witchcraft; tailor; costume designer; television commercial writer.

OTHER ELEMENTS

The remaining two elements, wood and metal, are from traditional Chinese palmistry. These are rare hand types and you won't see them very often, although it is important to recognize them when you do.

The Wood Hand

A wood hand (Figure 8.9) has gnarled, knobby knuckles and thin fingers with fine lines. Usually, the bones and tendons are prominent. This hand type is sometimes known in Western palmistry as the "philosopher's hand."

Wood types are thinkers; they are very facile with abstract thought. They love psychology, philosophy, and theories of human behavior. Over time, they develop their own spirituality by picking and choosing elements from several schools of thought to create an amalgam that is entirely their own. Woods love conversation and discussion, and are usually good in debates. Wood hands are often found on carpenters, craftspeople, and other people who are good with their hands. They tend to be physically active and have a broad outlook on life.

Woods do well with other wood types and water types (water gives nourishment to wood). Fire burns up wood though, so woods should avoid the fiery element, lest the relationship uses them up.

A wood type's karmic challenge is to learn as much as possible about the riddle of human existence and pass this wisdom on to others. Hence, woods make good

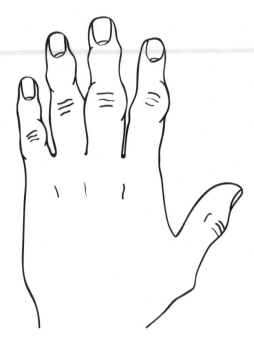

Figure 8.9—The wood hand

teachers and lecturers and often fulfill their karmic role in this way. However, wood types must be cautious not to lose themselves in endless speculation and elegant theories that look good on paper but have no practical value. They also must overcome a tendency to just "get by," and learn to use their talents productively. A lot of professional students are wood types.

Career: Philosopher, teacher, scientist, microbiologist, marine biologist, editor, researcher, proofreader, newspaper reporter, biographer, theoretical physicist, teacher of Eastern religious systems, critic.

The Metal Hand

The metal hand (Figure 8.10) is square—square palm, square fingertips, and square fingernails. The hand looks a bit like the earth hand but wirier, with a hard, angular surface. When you shake hands with a metal type, the first thing you notice is the hardness of the palm.

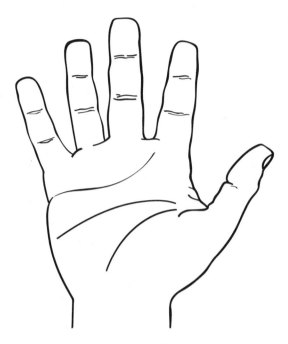

Figure 8.10—The metal hand

Metal types have a great work ethic. When the choice is between their personal needs and getting the job done, they pick the job every time. Strong-minded and a bit stubborn, metal types are hard to move from an opinion or attitude once they make up their mind. Usually, they are practical and realistic. This hand type is similar to the "practical or business hand" in Western palmistry.

Until the past couple of years, I never saw this type of hand. Metal types seek "practical" solutions to their problems, and often view fortune-telling with a skeptical eye. However, in recent years, psychic reading has gained a bit more credibility (even in the face of those awful 900-number hotlines!), and I see metal types occasionally. I don't see them as often as I see air and water types, but the numbers are growing. Metals almost always want to talk to me about work.

On the job, metal types are all business. Reliable, hard-working, and straightforward, metal types are ideal employees. They prefer to play by well-defined rules, and like an orderly environment. Away from work, metal types are friendly and personable. They never forget a favor, and will pay a good deed back with interest. Metal types like a balanced ledger. As independent thinkers, they rarely accept any new idea on trust alone. They must examine the new concept carefully and adapt it to their worldview. They get along well with others, although sometimes their strong opinions and honesty makes it hard for them to have close friends.

The karmic challenge for metal types is to learn to relax, slow down, and to enjoy the simple pleasures of life. They have to work at being flexible and seeing the other person's point of view. Both the iron pipe and the rapier are forged from metal, but the former is blunt and rigid while the latter is flexible and subtle. Often when metal types retire, they are financially capable of doing anything they want. The only problem is that, outside of work, they don't really know what to do with their time. The metal type has to learn that there's more to life than career, fame, and money.

Metal types should find their soul mates among other metals and among the free-flowing water types. The practical metal types do not get along well with the philosophical wood types. Remember, metal tries to chop away at wood, and dismisses the wood's speculations as impractical. Metal types focus on tangible reality while wood types deal with possibilities. Metal types also have problems with the intense fire types, as fire can melt metal. In other words, metal types can lose their identity in the cauldron of the fire type's intense passion. Air types tend to irritate metal types (just as air causes metal to rust) and this combination can be quite adversarial.

Career: Anything that makes a lot of money! Business, finance, real estate, law, banking, retail, stock exchange, investment, business ownership, landlord. Metals are also usually interested in martial arts.

Now that we've learned to distinguish the various elemental types of hands, we can proceed to the next step: comparing the elements of the hands.

Pain is a small thing. Life is a big thing.
You hurt a little. So what?

—My grandfather

chapter nine
BALANCING THE HAND TYPES

*Life is not a problem to be solved
but a reality to be experienced.*

—Kierkegaard, *Kierkegaard: A Biography*

Sometimes the left hand will be of one element and the right hand of another. In this case we must determine if the two elements are complementary or antagonistic. Obviously, if both hands are the same elemental type, the person has a well-integrated personality. This also applies if the two hands are different but complementary elements, although the personality will be more complex. Antagonistic elements, of course, produce conflict.

Certain elements complement each other and other elements do not. The rules for the four elements are:

Earth and water are complementary
Earth and fire are complementary
Fire and air are complementary
Earth and air are antagonistic

Water and air are antagonistic
Fire and water are antagonistic

We'll deal with the rarer elements, wood and metal, later on.

THE COMPLEMENTARY ELEMENTS

Earth and Water

If a person has a karmic (passive) earth hand and a social (dominant) water hand, the earth karma grounds the restless water spirit. Earth and water mixed together make clay, which is both firm and malleable. The earth/water type will be able to adapt to different social scenarios without ever losing sight of his or her true self.

If the karmic hand is a water type while the social hand is an earth type, you're looking at someone who is calm, controlled, and stable on the outside, but whose inner nature is restless, nervous, and experimental. The water/earth person may have grown up with a lot of social pressure, and may need encouragement to let his or her hair down and express some inner urges to explore new experiences. When properly expressed, the water/earth type has a disciplined free-floating creativity that makes it possible to call upon both right-brained (creative) forces as well as left-brained (logical) traits.

Career: Charity work; working with children; public service; paralegal; ear, nose, and throat specialist; agriculture; music; arts and crafts.

Fire and Air

When the karmic hand is a fire type and the social hand an air type, the burning intensity of the fire element is fanned by the imagination and mental power of the air element. This creates a powerful inventiveness, creative self-expression, independent thought process, and great passion in the person's chosen field.

If the karmic hand is an air type and the social hand fire, the person has been taught the importance of the phrase "Make something of yourself." Yet on the inside this person is more comfortable within the world of ideas and concepts. Air/fire types can be quite successful at their job, but whatever job they have must have meaning. For air/fire types to be fulfilled, they must have visible evidence of their success (i.e., money and security), but they must also commit themselves to an activity or profession that is useful and helpful to others. Their romantic idealism must be expressed in meaningful activities.

Career: Private investigator, reporter, humanitarian advocate, research assistant, clinical lab work, newspaper editor, any medical area, psychology and psychiatry, math and physics.

Earth and Fire

Oddly enough, it doesn't matter which hand is earth or which hand is fire. The end result of this mixture is the same, although the person gets there in different ways. Here, the stability of the earth element is combined with the intensity of fire to create a person who disciplines his or her ambition. These are usually self-made people who are able to focus on goals without losing themselves in their climb up the ladder of success. The natural impatience of fire is dampened by the cooling earth influence, which allows these types to build their success over time. If fire is in the karmic hand, the earth energy usually controls it through second thoughts; the person resists the initial impulsive urge and considers the consequences of the action. If fire is in the social hand, the person takes the conservative earth energy and boosts it to the next level with the fire power. Either way, the end result of these two powerful elements is the same: controlled passion.

Career: Mechanic, architect, engineer, computer programmer, movie special effects, real estate, political advisor, ecological causes, shaman.

THE ANTAGONISTIC ELEMENTS

Antagonistic elements create internal conflict that must be resolved in order for the person to find harmony and productivity. These karmic challenges are defined by the elements found in the two hands.

Earth and Air

The person with the antagonistic elements of earth and air in the hands must learn to balance the intellectual energy of air with the practical demands of earth.

Air is the stronger element, so the practical earth energy may get blown away by the air's tendency to chase impractical dreams.

If the karmic hand is earth, this person was meant to have a simpler life than he or she probably actually has. The earth's strong sense of responsibility causes this type to take on too much, which causes the social hand to take on airlike qualities. Burnout can definitely be a problem, as earth/air people will eventually reach their limit, throw their hands in the air, and say, "Forget it!"

If the karmic hand is air and the social hand is earth, then the person may have been taught to seek out routine jobs and financial security at the sacrifice of his or her freedom. I see air/earth types as being raised in the Pavlovian tradition; conditioned to automatically do the right thing, follow the rules, and don't make a fuss. However, the repressed water energy longs for freedom of expression, and these people will feel a sort of aimless restlessness until they allow their energy to flow freely.

Often, this type has a midlife change of direction from a traditional, conservative job to something more glamorous and self-expressive. One of my clients, an air/earth type, was a corporate lawyer who, at the age of fifty, quit his job and became a painter. He told me that his wife thought he was crazy, but he was a lot happier and his blood pressure went down twenty points.

Career: Hospitality (restaurant and bar), dietary counseling, veterinarian, history and social sciences, antiques, anthropology, restoration.

Water and Air

Water and air are antagonistic. If the karmic hand is water, the biggest problem of this mixture is the tendency to fritter away time and energy on projects that have no chance of paying off. The superior air element of the social hand can overcome the water's desire to accomplish things, which leads these types to constantly talk themselves out of doing things that might actually be great ideas.

Air in the karmic hand leads to a similar, but more difficult problem. These people have a double dose of "living in their own head." Their challenge is to take the rich dream-life of their thoughts and ideas and make them real. Often, they must first form a partnership with a more grounded earth or metal type to make this happen. They are constantly talking about all the great ideas they have that will make them rich someday, and most of these ideas are excellent, but they seldom act on them. With a little help, though, these dreams can be made real.

Career: Librarian, managing museums and collections, critic, editor, proofreader, quality control supervisor, career counselor, guidance counselor, chef, bartender.

Fire and Water

Fire and water are the two most volatile elements when brought together. Fire in the karmic hand and water in the social hand creates a combination so overcharged with energy, and with so many activities going at once, that this type risks burnout. A person with this combination will try to do everything. Often, fire/water people suffer from nervous disorders and insomnia. They are extremely driven, so it's essential that they learn to slow down and budget their time, money, and energy.

When water is in the karmic hand, it makes the person sensitive to criticism. A water/fire's feelings can be easily hurt. On the other hand, praise and recognition will make water/fire people strive to outdo themselves. Other challenges include learning to control their temper and developing patience with those who are less driven than they.

Career: Medicine, painting, sculpture, policeperson, pharmacologist, dancer, martial artist, military, stock broker, banker.

THE RARER ELEMENTS

Now we get into those rarer elements, metal and wood. These are some of the most interesting and unusual people in the world, and always make for a challenging read! The rules are:

Metal and water are complementary
Wood and water are complementary
Wood and earth are complementary
Wood and fire are antagonistic
Wood and metal are antagonistic
Metal and fire are antagonistic

Metal and Water

The complementary elements of metal and water make an extremely powerful combination. When metal is in the karmic hand and water is in the social hand, the person is usually extroverted, brash, and flamboyant. Metal/water types enjoy being the center of attention. Since water types can take any form, they're natural mimics. The metal element can add a sharp edge to this wit, and turn it a bit sarcastic. Even at an early age the metal/water's sense of humor and ability to do imitations makes itself known. In school, they sometimes get in trouble for imitating the teacher or principal.

Metal/water types must learn to be aware of the effect they have on others. Sometimes they'll say or do things that strike them as appropriate or amusing, and do not understand that they sometimes leave hurt feelings behind them. "Don't be so sensitive!" they admonish others. Once they learn compassion, however, this trait disappears.

Water in the karmic hand and metal in the social hand creates a type who can take charge of a madhouse. They keep track of all the myriad responsibilities and functions of running organized chaos. Water/metal types know how to motivate others, and bring out the best in anyone. Often, they see hidden potential in others that nobody else suspects, and are very good at encouraging the hidden gift to blossom.

As incredibly fast learners, water/metal types rise quickly up the ladder of success. Unfortunately, once they achieve their goal, they often get bored with it and want to move on to a greater challenge. However, if they stick with their goals, there's no limit to how high they can climb.

Career: College professor, science teacher, lawyer, ethics, public speaking, pediatrician, dentist, comedian, actor, songwriter.

Wood and Water

Wood and water are complementary elements, so the person with this combination gets the best of both worlds. Wood gives the person a deep-rooted sense of self, while the water element blesses him or her with freedom of expression. Socially versatile, wood/water types are at home in blue jeans or full evening dress. In all aspects of their life, they enjoy a broad range of activity. Musically, they'll enjoy everything from rock 'n' roll to symphonies; gastronomically, they'll eat anything from hotdogs to haute cuisine; literarily, they'll read both comic books and Shakespeare; and philosophically, they'll explore many avenues of thought. Wood/water types can talk to anybody about anything, and are masters of games where knowledge of trivia is important.

Water/wood types seem to be the same as wood/water types, but my experience has shown they are a little more secretive. They can talk to you for hours about tin production in Bolivia, or any number of subjects, but reveal very little about themselves. However, at the end of the conversation they'll have learned a lot about you!

Career: Teacher, philosopher, priest, preacher, principal, coach, game show host, chiropractor, orthopedic surgeon, TV producer, beautician, scriptwriter, photographer.

Wood and Earth

Wood/earth types are almost invariably self-motivators, self-starters, and self-made people. Just don't expect them to make quick decisions! The philosophical wood element likes to weigh options, balancing the pros and cons of each decision. If you try to hurry them, the stubborn earth element takes over and you might as well be talking to the wall.

When wood is in the karmic hand and earth is in the social, the person will build his or her future over time, deferring immediate satisfaction for a greater reward somewhere over the horizon. Wood/earth types are great planners, and they like to drive their roots deep into whatever they're doing. Although they often wonder if they're making the right decisions, the test of time proves that they almost always follow the correct course of action. If you want practical solutions to complicated problems, the wood/earth type is the perfect person to ask.

When earth is found in the karmic hand and wood is in the social hand, the person will have a frank, open approach to life. While naive in youth, earth/wood types quickly learn about the ways of the world. Their early idealism becomes tempered into a firm resolve to get as much from life as they can in the time allotted.

Career: Professional student, agriculture, gardening, forestry, husbandry, veterinarian, child care, plastic or reconstructive surgeon, carpenter/stonemason, clothes designer, jewelry maker, interpreter.

Wood and Fire

Since these two hand types are so different (wood is knobby and fire is fleshy), I must admit that I've never seen this combination. However, if I ever do, I'll know that the wood/fire combination must overcome a tendency to be his or her own worst enemy. Fire devours wood, so these types will tend to eat away at their self with self-doubt, negativity, and a defeatist attitude. Yet, if they can learn to balance the wood/fire relationship, they should be able to cultivate the passion of fire while avoiding the conflict between wood and fire. Still, self-doubt will be a constant obstacle that they will have to learn to manage and overcome.

Career: The wood element gives the person a predisposition toward philosophy and the study of the human condition, while the fire gives passion, ambition, and impatience. It seems to me that fire/wood types would be attracted to careers that demand a lot of energy and thought. I can see them as musicians who rise quickly to the top of their field and then lose it all; poets who try to change the world with their verse but never make a dime at it; scientists who develop a new means of waging war; writers of great literature of such devastating pessimism that nobody enjoys reading it. The problem is that in a battle between wood and fire, fire usually wins. The wood element eventually is consumed.

However, I don't think any situation is hopeless, and this applies to the wood/fire combination. Since the wood/fire combination runs a great risk toward self-destruction, the person must take every precaution against self-destructive behavior. I think great things could be accomplished through the energy generated by the conflict between these two elements, as long as the fire is controlled and the blaze moderated.

As I mentioned earlier, I've never seen this combination and I'm not sure that it can even exist, but anything's possible.

Wood and Metal

Wood and metal are antagonistic, and I've seen two examples of this combination in the past ten years. This is a very rare combination. The biggest problem with this combination is that metal always wants to be in charge. Fire, however, is so impatient that it doesn't want to wait long enough to work its way to the top.

Wood in the karmic hand and metal in the social hand indicates a person who faces the world aggressively and maintains a "me-against-the-world" attitude. The will power of metal combines with the rationalizing ability of wood to make the person defensive and hard to reason with. He or she is always right, and will not discuss the issue. The term "all-purpose expert" applies here with a vengeance.

When metal is in the karmic hand and wood is in the social hand, the person has the same sense of "rightness," but develops an incredible framework of rationalizations against what appears to be a hostile and unappreciative world. In other words, this person is never to blame, and it's always someone else's fault.

I recall doing a reading for a metal/wood type about six years ago. He told me that he seemed to have problems keeping a job. Every time he got comfortable with a situation, "somebody would do something to screw it up for me." During the course of our conversation, it became evident that *he* was the one with the problem. His aggressive approach made others uncomfortable around him. Furthermore, he always tried to second-guess the boss's decisions. "My boss was an idiot," he told me when I pointed this out to him.

From his point of view, he was constantly the victim of circumstances beyond his control. He had been sabotaged by jealous coworkers, accused of spreading false rumors ("I never told a lie in my life!"), and persecuted by moronic bosses. His explanations for his misfortune were brilliant, and completely absolved himself of any blame.

Bearing in mind that nobody is a helpless victim of fate or karma, I knew that he could change his behavior with a little effort. No one is doomed from birth to live out their dispositions. A little firm parenting would have taught him to take responsibility for his tendency to blame others. I asked him about his childhood. Unfortunately, he was raised by parents who always made excuses for him. Not once did he ever have to suffer the consequences of his actions. Furthermore, he still lived with his mother, who encouraged his tendency to blame others by telling him that others were jealous of his looks and intelligence.

Did he ever get better? I do not know. I talked to him at length about personal responsibility and learning to work with others. He tuned all this out, and continually returned to the question, "Why does everyone feel threatened by me?" I did the best I could for him and encouraged him to come back if he needed. I never saw him again.

Career: Fiction writer, movie critic, food and beverage industry, mathematics, physics, engineering, merchandising, manufacturing, fashion design.

Metal and Fire

Antagonistic elements metal and fire can create a person with incredible passion and indomitable will. People with metal in the karmic hand may have little compassion or sense of ethics. Nothing will stand between them and their goal. I imagine someone like Napoleon or Alexander the Great were metal/fire types. Metal/fire people must learn compassion, and to recognize the consequences of their actions.

When fire is in the karmic hand and metal is in the social hand, the same sense of burning purpose and determination exists. However, with a little spiritual work, fire/metal types can be a great asset to the human race. Coming to terms with their inner conflict creates a tremendous understanding of the conflicts around them. They passionately follow their personal vision, bringing the metal's sense of determination to bear on the business of making their vision real.

Both metal/fire and fire/metal types have the power to change the world. If their vision is to bend the world to their will (like Napoleon and Alexander the Great), they will try to do so with all their fire power. If, however, their vision is more spiritual, you have a Gandhi or Mohammed on your hands—people who burn with a great spiritual vision and who have the unbendable determination of the warrior to overcome evil.

Career: Spiritual leader, specialized surgery, chemistry, urban renewal, missionary, import/export, endocrinology, dermatology, author, poet, motivational speaker.

> *The power of choosing good and evil*
> *is within the reach of all.*
>
> —Origen, *The Commentaries*

chapter ten
OTHER HAND SHAPES & USEFUL KARMIC SIGNS

> As for palmistry . . . such chiromancy is not
> only reprobated by theologians, but by men of
> law and physics and science as a false, foolish,
> vain, scandalous, futile, superstitious practice,
> smelling much of divinery and pacts with the
> devil . . .
>
> —Torreblanca, *The Zincali*

There are certain hand shapes that combine the classical elements into a rec-
ognizably unique form. When we see these shapes, it provides us with a
"shorthand" method of classifying the type. Below are a few of the most common
hand types I've found in my practice.

THE CONIC HAND

From the system of hand classification invented by D'Arpentigny, the conic hand
(Figure 10.1) is a very beautiful type. This almond-shaped hand represents a
refined, sensitive, and empathic person. As a variation of the water hand, a true

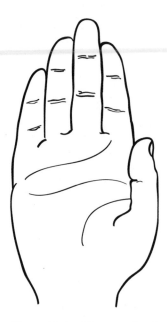

Figure 10.1—The conic hand

conic hand should have a smooth curve, finely textured skin, and tapering finger-tips. On a male it indicates a sympathetic, sensitive, and intuitive outlook—not your average "macho" type! Male conic types find that the best friends for them are women.

People possessing a conic hand seem to always attract the personal confessions of others. This causes me to sometimes think of it as the "Dear Abby hand."

Conic types are sensitive to their environment. They can be described as emotional barometers; they feel happy around happy people, tired and anxious around negative people, and threatened by hostile people. Like most water types, conic types can become overburdened with responsibilities. This is most often caused by the myriad needy people they seem to collect.

The karmic need for conic types is that it's vital for them to learn to set aside time for their own needs. I find that if they discharge their drive to help others in a job that satisfies this need—nursing, counseling, physical therapy, and so on—they learn to do this. Otherwise, they run the danger of giving their lives to other

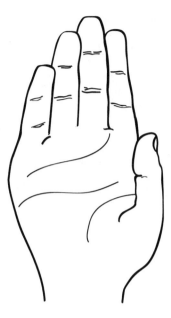

Figure 10.2—The spatulate hand

people in bits and pieces without receiving anything in return. Conic types are very, very giving, and they must take care not to let others take advantage of this caring nature.

THE SPATULATE HAND

The spatulate hand is easy to spot because the palm of the hand looks like a spatula—wider at one end than the other (Figure 10.2). True spatulate hands will have splayed fingertips as well. If the hand is a water type with long fingers and a long palm, the person has an excess of internal energy and is always on the go. If the hand is an air type (square palm, long fingers), the person tends to be a bit nervous, fantasy-prone, and at times unrealistic. Air spatulates make great actors and actresses because of their ability to make-believe. I call them "shape-shifters" and they usually agree. Earth spatulates (square palm, short fingers) are extremely energetic, amiable outdoor types, like Steve Irwin, the extroverted host of *The Crocodile Hunter*. Fire spatulates (long palm, short fingers) are restless, idealistic, and changeable. They are often found running from one interest to the next. They throw themselves into the new interest with a passion, and then leave it for another, more fascinating activity. Unfortunately, they often do the same thing in relationships. However, if they find a field of endeavor that provides them with a constant, ever-changing challenge, they'll embrace it as their life work.

The biggest karmic need of spatulate types, in my experience, is that whatever they do in life must have meaning. Not satisfied with just making a living, spatulate types must feel that their work serves a higher purpose. Otherwise, they begin to ask, "Is this all there is to life?" and move on. Empowerment and self-expression are important factors in their happiness too.

The spatulate personality reminds me of a passage from Meister Eckhart, which I have modernized slightly:

> The kind of work we do
> does not make us holy
> but we can make it holy.
> However "sacred"
> a calling may be,
> as a calling
> it has no power to sanctify;
> but rather as we are and have
> the divine being within,
> we bless each task we do . . .
> be it eating, or sleeping,
> or watching, or any other.
> Whatever they do,
> those who have not
> much of God's nature,
> they work in vain.[‡]

Amen, good Meister, amen.

[‡]Oliver Davies, trans., *Meister Eckhart: Selected Writings* (New York: Penguin Books, 1994), 7–8.

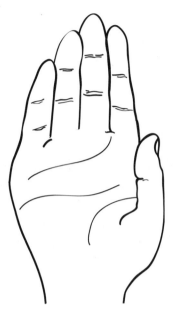

Figure 10.3—The diamond hand

THE DIAMOND HAND

The diamond hand is a variation of the spatulate hand. With a triangular palm and tapered fingers (Figure 10.3), the hand takes on a distinct diamond shape. Diamond types love luxury, money, expensive things, clothes, and jewelry. However, they can be very careful shoppers and tight with money. They like to get value for their dollar.

Diamond types are social creatures who love to dance and mingle. I see them a lot when I work fundraisers; they are usually dressed to the nines and with an impeccable hairstyle. Male or female, diamond types are very conscious of their appearance.

Diamond types are usually quite intelligent, have refined tastes, and love good food, good wine, and good conversation. Like all spatulates, they love variety. They usually know a lot about art, current events, and the latest styles. They have their finger on the pulse of the world around them, and have an uncanny instinct for what the best thing to do would be under almost any situation. I suspect that in an immediate past life, most diamond types were royalty.

The karmic need of diamond types is to avoid shallowness and not become totally focused on material pleasures. Diamond types have a tendency to turn a blind eye on unpleasantness, and often must experience a "wake-up call" in the form of having their noses rubbed in human suffering to develop an understanding of what's important in life.

KARMIC SIGNS IN THE HAND

There are certain line formations found in the hand that have special meanings. Below are a few of my favorites.

Jacob's Ladder

I love to see this sign (Figures 10.4 and 10.4A) because it means the person for whom I am reading will take what I say, evaluate it, and apply it to his or her own growth. Jacob's Ladder is a sign that the person will be constantly growing in a spiritual sense, whittling away at his or her karmic debt and learning whatever lessons need to be learned. It is one sign of the self-taught person.

Jacob's Ladder is formed by a series of "rungs" connecting the fate line and another line—sometimes it connects to a secondary fate line, as shown in Figure 10.4, and at other times it connects the fate line and the life line. People with this sign are constantly upwardly mobile, and push aggressively through whatever challenges life throws at them. I consider them highly evolved souls who have learned many, many lessons.

The Pagoda

The Pagoda (Figures 10.5 and 10.5A) looks a lot like Jacob's Ladder except the two "uprights" of the ladder are not parallel, but tilt toward each other. Like Jacob's Ladder, the Pagoda is a sign that the person is concerned with spiritual growth, but in this case his or her best path to growth is through the studies of Buddhist or Zen Buddhist teachings.

People with the Pagoda are usually extremely talented at teaching and explaining the conundrums of life to others. At times I've wondered if perhaps the person with the Pagoda is only a few lifetimes away from becoming an ascended master.

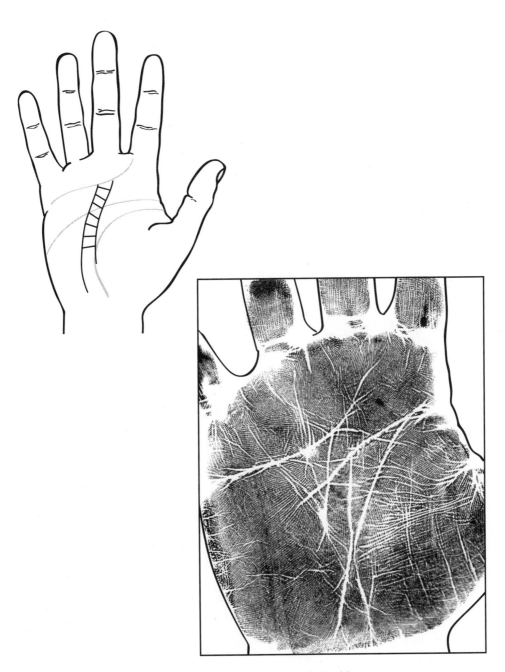

Figures 10.4 and 10.4A—Jacob's Ladder

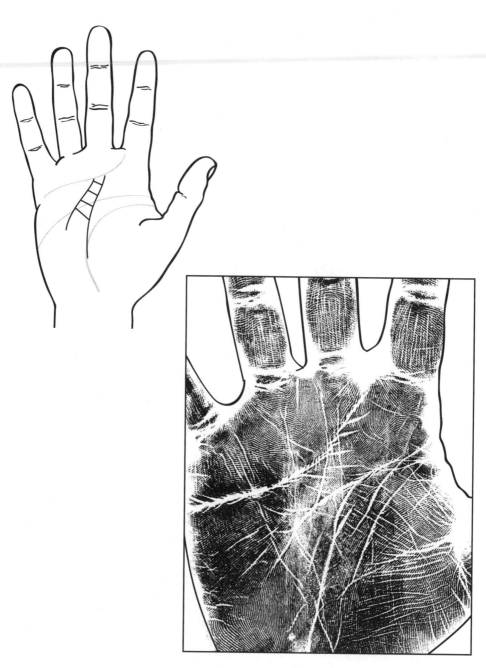

Figures 10.5 and 10.5A—The Pagoda

Saint George's Shield

Saint George's Shield is a special symbol (Figures 10.6 and 10.6A) that looks like a shield with a large cross on it. It can be found virtually anywhere in the hand where enough lines intersect to form it. Saint George is one of those historical figures about whom a great many legends have arisen, the best known of which is the Golden Legend.

According to the Golden Legend, there was a dragon that lived in a lake in Libya and terrorized the neighboring villages. Whole armies had gone up against this fierce creature to no avail. The dragon had a voracious appetite, and to placate the beast the villagers fed it two sheep each day. Eventually the dragon depleted the local supply of mutton and the townspeople began drawing lots to see who next would be the dragon's dinner. As was common in those days, maidens were substituted for sheep. The dragon didn't seem to mind, and devoured the maidens just as eagerly as he had the sheep.

During this last extremity, Saint George rode into the village. Discovering that a princess was about to be eaten by the hungry dragon, George made the sign of the cross, rode to battle against the serpent, and killed it with a single blow of his lance. In the aftermath of this victory, George converted the locals to Christianity. The king of the village, overcome with gratitude at having his daughter back, presented the brave knight with a large reward. Saint George immediately distributed the cash to the poor and rode off.

When found in the palm of the hand, the Shield of Saint George indicates a person who is a crusader against injustice. He or she has an instinctive dislike for injustice, unfairness, and oppression of the helpless. Often, this person becomes involved in charitable causes, including those that benefit animals and exploited or abused children.

People bearing this sign who explore their past lives often see themselves as wandering knights, soldiers, and defenders of the weak. Quite often, there is a direct karmic connection to the Order of the Knights Templar and the Rosicrucians.

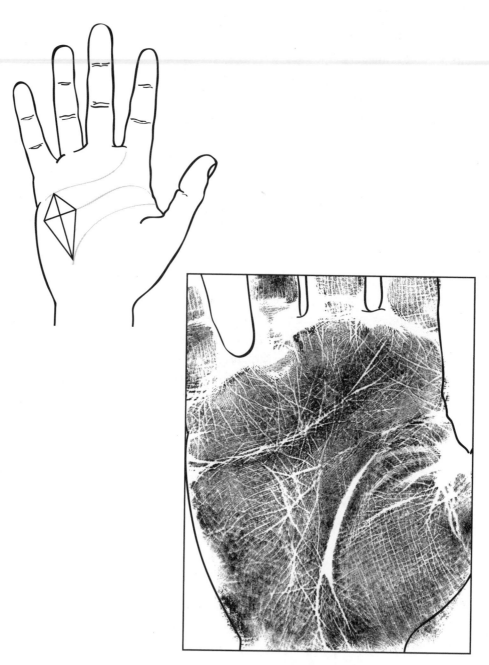

Figures 10.6 and 10.6A—Saint George's Shield

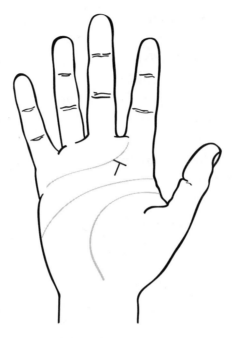

Figure 10.7—The Nail

The Nail

The Nail (Figure 10.7) is a figure that looks like a clear, dark letter *T*. It indicates a recurring obstacle that we keep encountering in our life with which we have to learn to deal. The lesson of the Nail is that we cannot conquer this particular obstacle through force or will power alone. We must learn to work with the obstacle until we figure out a way around it. Some people actually manage to turn the obstacle into an asset through clever thinking.

When pursuing a dream, it's not uncommon to discover that the closer we get to our goal, the more obstacles we encounter. It's like the universe (or karma?) is testing our resolve. "How badly do you want this?", it seems to ask. "What are you willing to go through to realize this dream?" Over time, these obstacles begin to seem familiar; and they should, as they all spring from a common source: your Nail.

My own "Nail" is lack of planning and poor time management. As soon as I think I'm out of the woods and the brass ring is within my grasp, my poor planning catches up with me. I encounter car problems, computer crashes, or a lack of money, all of which are caused by the same Nail. I've learned to deal with these minor setbacks amiably while keeping my eye on the final goal, but learning this lesson took a lot of time and energy.

Usually a Nail is correctable with diligent self-discipline, but sometimes it isn't, as in the case of a physical infirmity or handicap. Also, the location of the Nail can give us a clue as to the area we're most likely to encounter the problem. If found on the mount under the forefinger, it indicates a challenge involving issues of control and self-esteem. If found under the second finger, it can mean the challenge will involve moral issues.

A Nail under the third finger can indicate a frustrated or incompletely manifested creative urge. In other words, the flow of creative energy is blocked. When found under the little finger, the Nail can indicate challenges involving relationships—usually one arising from a lack of communication between the parties.

Sometimes, a Nail will be found on the Mount of Venus (the large pad of the thumb). This can indicate challenges of a sexual nature. These people will have to learn to balance their sex drive with the other factors of their life. Sometimes the challenge involves repressed sexuality yearning to be released instead. Sometimes it can mean the other extreme: decisions made because of a powerful sexual attraction to another person that may temporarily blind us to their faults.

Seal of the Lotus

The Lotus is a six- or eight-pointed sign that looks just like an asterisk (Figures 10.8 and 10.8A). It's a sign that you will be tested throughout your life, but you will pass your tests if you act correctly. Like a lot of principles of Eastern thought, it is a blessing with a negative side: yes, you will pass your tests, but doesn't this also mean that you will be tested? These tests are never, ever easy.

I think the Lotus teaches us about the proper use of our creative and mental forces. It's easy to misdirect our energy into unrewarding activities. Distracted by the demands of our daily existence—the pursuit of money, power, prestige, security, love—we lose sight of the important questions: "Who am I?", "What is the purpose of my life?", and "What can I give back to the Universe in payment for my life?" Unfortunately, no amount of success or wealth can appease the longing

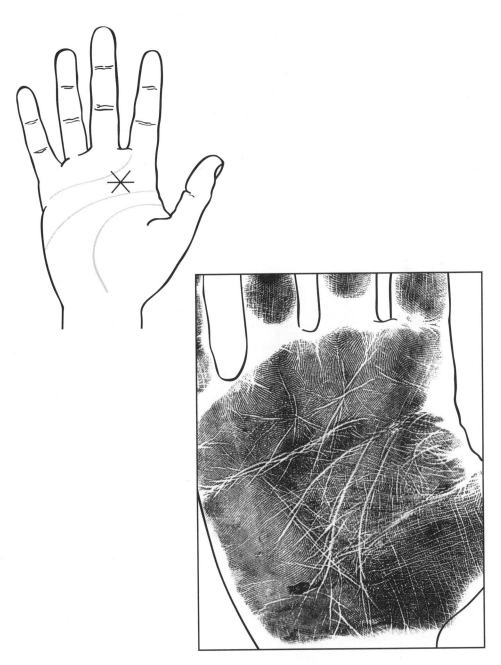

Figures 10.8 and 10.8A—The Seal of the Lotus

of the spirit to rid itself from the burden of karmic debt. If we're not diligently working toward becoming the sum of our potential, we're not learning the karmic lessons we *must* learn. We'll feel a nagging inside our spirit; a restlessness, depression, and a lack of direction. We'll lose our sense of purpose, which is why job burnout is so common it has been described as an epidemic.

Like the Nail, the location of the Lotus can give us a clue as to which area of our life the tests are most likely to arise. When it's under the forefinger, it means that our self-image and confidence may be tested; under the second finger, we may find our sense of purpose tested; under the third finger, it's our creativity that will be tested; and under the pinky finger, our communication and relationship skills will be tested. However, unlike the Nail, which represents an obstacle we have to learn to live with, the Lotus shows us that we can pass these tests with direct, assertive action.

The Lotus reminds us that we grow through struggle. If our work ceases to be challenging, or if we quit testing our limits, we're not growing; and when we're not growing, we're dying.

> *You cannot bring the mountain-top to the valley. If you would attain to the mountain-top you must pass through the valley, climb the steeps, unafraid of the dangerous precipices.*
>
> —Jiddhu Krishnamurti, *Talk 1: Direct Perceptions and Transformations*

chapter eleven

THE EIGHT TRIGRAMS
OF THE I CHING

*Seek not happiness too greedily,
and be not fearful of happiness.*

—Lao Tsu, *Tao te Ching*

The Yijing, or as it's commonly known, I Ching, is to Chinese culture what the Bible is to Christian culture. The term *I Ching* means "Book of Changes," and refers to the belief that everything is in a constant flux of transformation from one state of being to another. It's difficult to say exactly how old the I Ching is, but we know that Confucius considered it an ancient book over 2,500 years ago. Legend has it that the first emperor of China, Fu-Hsi, discovered the Changes more than six thousand years ago. By any account, the book is very, very old.

About three thousand years ago, King Wen designed the sixty-four hexagrams of the I Ching and assigned names to them. He is said to have done this while languishing in prison at the hands of Chou Hsin, king of the Shang. The sixty-four hexagrams of the I Ching diagram every possible set of changes.

Briefly, a *change* is a transition from a yang state to a yin state, or vice versa. *Yang* means "sunny side of the mountain," and represents activity, creativity, the

137

conscious, and the here and now. *Yin* means "dark side of the mountain," and represents what's gone, passive, unconscious, reactive, or inactive.

A *hexagram* is a layout of six yin or yang symbols representing six levels of a situation. From bottom to top the levels are matter, energy, instinct, human emotion, mind, and wisdom. After Wen's death, his son, the Duke of Chou, completed his father's work.

Although there were apparently many versions of the Book of Changes, only the one written by the Duke of Chou, with an extensive commentary by Confucius, has survived to this day. The Book of Changes has been translated many, many times. Where palmistry enters the picture is that the sixty-four hexagrams are constructed from eight trigrams, or lines of three changes. In traditional Chinese palmistry, these eight trigrams can be found in the palm!

Since the lessons of the I Ching instruct us how to respond to a particular life challenge, is it too far a reach to assume that the hexagrams currently active in our hands tell us what karmic lesson we're currently facing and how to properly deal with it? Wouldn't it be wonderful if all we had to do to discover our current karmic challenges and lessons was to look at the palms of our own hands?

If this idea appeals to you, keep reading!

To learn to use this fascinating method of divination, you must have a copy of the I Ching handy. Those of you who are already familiar with the Book of Changes can go right ahead with this method with no further preparation. I wanted to keep this book complete in itself, so if you're new to the I Ching, there's no need to have to buy another book in order to use the information contained in this chapter. For your convenience, I've included a down-and-dirty interpretation of the I Ching in the next chapter. My synopsis will be enough to get you started, but if you want to go further, I recommend any of the several excellent interpretations of the I Ching mentioned in the bibliography.

I warn you that this is a rather complicated method of divination, but the rewards of learning it are well worth the effort. First, let's look at the trigrams.

THE EIGHT TRIGRAMS

The eight trigrams and their meanings are:

Ch'ien

THE CREATIVE

Element: Heaven, sky

Attribute: Strength, creativity

Animal: Horse

Direction: Northwest

Chen

THE AROUSING

Element: Thunder

Attribute: Movement, initiative, action, education

Animal: Dragon

Direction: East

K'an

THE ABYSMAL

Element: Water, moon, the deep

Attribute: Danger

Animal: Pig

Direction: North

Ken

KEEPING STILL

Element: Mountain

Attribute: Stillness, stopping

Animal: Dog

Direction: Northeast

K'un
THE RECEPTIVE

Element: Earth   *Animal:* Ox
Attribute: Docility, receptivity   *Direction:* Southwest

Li
THE CLINGING

Element: Sun, fire   *Animal:* Pheasant
Attribute: Brightness, Fame   *Direction:* South

Sun
THE GENTLE

Element: Wind, wood   *Animal:* Fowl
Attribute: Penetration, following, wealth   *Direction:* Southeast

Tui
THE JOYOUS

Element: Lake, mist, marsh   *Animal:* Sheep
Attribute: Pleasure, joy, attraction   *Direction:* West

Don't try to memorize the trigrams, just take a few moments to familiarize your-self with them, bearing in mind that each set of three lines represents changes from a yin state to a yang state or vice versa. This will be important later.

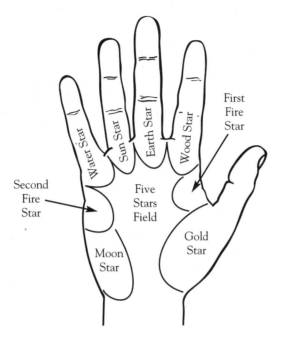

Figure 11.1—The nine stars of Chinese palmistry

THE NINE STARS

The areas in the hands containing the trigrams correspond to the fleshy areas Western palmists call the *mounts*. In Chinese palmistry, these areas are called *stars*, and are identified as shown in Figure 11.1. The stars are interpreted just as the mounts are in Western palmistry; they are examined closely for size, color, and the presence of lines or markings. A well-developed star that is free of negative signs is an omen of good luck in the area ruled by that particular star. A well-developed star can be identified by either of two signs: a high center (like a small hill) or a single, strong vertical line. If the area has a lot of grilles, crossbars, or crosses, or is too flat, it is a passive star.

The center of the star is agreed to be the point where we find a triangular skin-ridge pattern called the *triradius* (Figure 11.2). We examine the high point of the star to see if it is to the left or right of the triradius when we construct the hexagram. This determines the changing lines in the I Ching. We'll talk more about this later.

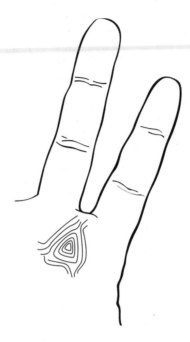

Figure 11.2—Triradius

Western palmistry teaches us that the mounts represent the activities that give us the greatest sense of satisfaction. Could it be that we enjoy these activities because they correspond with our karmic tasks? If so, then the stars provide an extremely useful tool to identify those activities that help us discharge our karmic debt. The interpretation of each star is as follows.

The Wood Star corresponds with the Jupiter Mount in Western palmistry and represents independence, control, personal development, self-awareness, and leadership. The Chinese associate this star with the development of the personality.

The Earth Star corresponds to the Saturn Mount and represents teaching, discipline, and a refined sense of morality. In Chinese palmistry, it is also associated with determination.

The Sun Star corresponds to the Apollo Mount and is associated with creativity, design, the arts, literature, science, and optimism. Well-developed Sun Stars indicate sunny people who are happy and outgoing. The Chinese associate the Sun Star with success.

The Water Star corresponds to the Mercury Mount and represents independence of expression, communication, shrewdness, adaptability, and charm. The Chinese also associate the Water Star with the acquisition of money.

The Fire Stars correspond to the Upper and Lower Mounts of Mars. The First Fire Star represents aggression. When firm and well developed, it can indicate a self-starter. When poorly developed, it can indicate someone who looks to others for motivation.

The Second Fire Star represents courage, and the ability to defend ourselves and stand up for what we believe in. When firm and well developed, it gives the person the strength of his or her convictions. When poorly developed, the person can be a bit wishy-washy.

In Western palmistry, Mars has three faces: Upper Mars, Lower Mars, and the Plain of Mars. The Plain of Mars corresponds to the Five Stars Field. When firm and strong, this gives the person wisdom, common sense, and an even temperament. When weak or flabby, the person may lack self-confidence. People with a weak Five Stars Field often have problems recognizing their own gifts, and do not always act in their own best interest. In other words, they need guidance.

The Gold Star corresponds to the Mount of Venus and represents yang energy, the libido, and the way the subject expresses his or her love. A large Gold Star indicates a strong sex drive, a strong ability to show physical affection, and a bright outlook on life.

The Moon Star corresponds with the Luna Mount and relates to the passive yin energy, as well as intuition, psychic development, and the ability to sense danger in a situation.

THE EIGHT PALMAR TRIGRAMS

Figure 11.3 shows the locations of the eight trigrams on the palm. Notice that most of them fall near one of the stars. The exceptions are the Sun Star, which has no trigram associated with it, and the Gold Star, which has two trigrams associated with it: Chen and Ken. The latter two correspond to the Mounts of Vulcan and Venus, respectively.

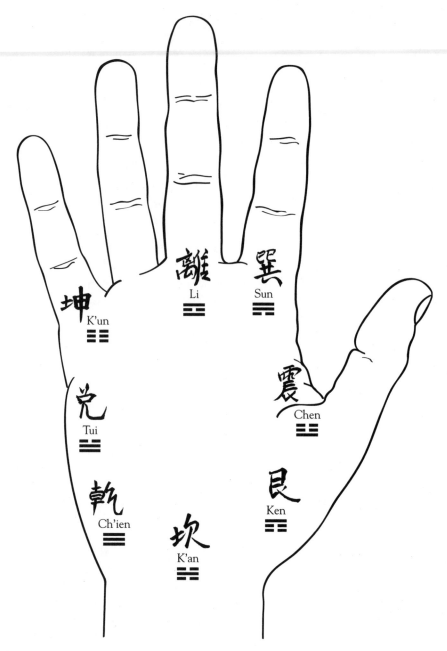

Figure 11.3—The locations of the eight trigrams on the palm

To determine which trigram is the most active at the present time, we look for the largest, most developed star (mount). It is important to check the stars regularly, as they can, and do, change over time.

For example, my fullest, most developed star is Wood, which is located beneath the forefinger. The trigram for the Wood Star is Sun:

Sun indicates prosperity and success at self-directed business ventures. Synchronistically enough, the time of this writing also happens to be my numerological eight year, which means the same thing.

My second most well-developed star is Water, which contains the trigram K'un:

The Water Star controls the flow of ideas and communication, and the K'un trigram indicates receptiveness, empathy, and understanding. These are the attributes that, according to the oracle, will contribute most to my success.

If we combine the two trigrams (putting the first trigram on the bottom), we form a hexagram:

(*Note:* Hexagrams are read from bottom to top.) This can now be looked up in the I Ching and used for divinatory purposes! In the above example, my hexagram is number 46, Sheng. Sheng is composed of wood at the bottom and earth at the top, which represents the upward push of the tree through the nurturing earth. According to the I Ching, Sheng indicates upward movement accomplished through great effort. The text of the I Ching emphasizes this upward movement is not accomplished through aggressiveness but through modesty and adaptability. A good omen indeed!

COMPLETING THE READING

To complete the reading, you can perform a coin or yarrow stick divination using the I Ching and gain further insights into the situation. I prefer to use a dowsing procedure that creates a prognostication from the hand with the aid of a pendulum.

First, a little theory: Imagine that the star areas are constantly shifting from a yin (flat and inactive) state to a yang (round and active) state, and then back again, just as everything in the universe rises and falls from the ultimate Source. It requires a significant amount of energy to cause the tissue of the hand to change shape, so we can assume that this energy builds up for a while before manifesting itself as a visible change. These pools of energy, which I believe are created by the body's ch'i (life energy), fall in line with the acupuncture meridians of the hand (Figure 11.4) and can be easily detected with a pendulum.

To begin, hold the subject's hand in a horizontal position, palm up. Support the weight of his or her hand in yours from below. Hold the pendulum in a relaxed grip in your other hand. The tip of the pendulum should be held about two inches from the surface of the subject's palm. Place your mind in a passive, receptive state, and slowly move the pendulum from star to star, holding it above each star for a few seconds to see if anything happens. Signs that you're over a high-energy area are twitching of the pendulum's tip, a circular motion over the star, or a trembling vibration that shakes the pendulum. This latter energy is so strong that you can often get a reading from a fresh hand print!

Construct a hexagram from the two strongest changing stars and interpret as you did before. This procedure predicts the changes from the subject's current situation to one immediately in his or her future. If the subject is familiar with the use of the pendulum, sometimes it is better to let the subject dowse his or her own hand and construct the hexagram.

FOR ADVANCED READERS: DETERMINING THE CHANGING LINES

To take full advantage of the I Ching's divinatory applications, we have to determine which of the lines of the palmar hexagram are *changing* lines. The changing lines determine which lines of each hexagram applies to the current situation.

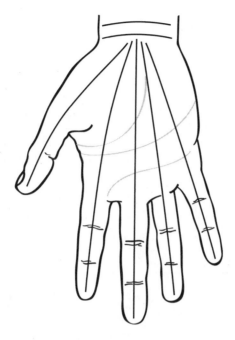

Figure 11.4—The acupuncture meridians of the hand

To break down each one of the palmar trigrams into stable and changing lines, we use a variation of the three-coin divination applied to the stars. First, we locate the apex of the star. As we learned earlier, this is the point where the dermal ridges form a small triangle called the triradius. Once we locate the apex, we divide the mount into three sections, with the width of the triradius as the center section (Figure 11.5). The width of the star (or mount) is determined by how far the lines define a triangle before falling apart into the surrounding whorl patterns. If the lines of the hand are extrafine and hard to read, I find it helps a great deal to dust the area with a brush lightly dipped in dark eye shadow.

Figures 11.5 and 11.6 show the Water Star between the ring and little fingers. The trigram for the Water Star is K'un (☷). To determine if the center (ruling) line of the trigram is changing or stable, we must determine if the apex of the star is truly its highest elevation. If it is, the center line of the trigram is stable. If it isn't, then the center line of the trigram is changing. Other factors that determine the

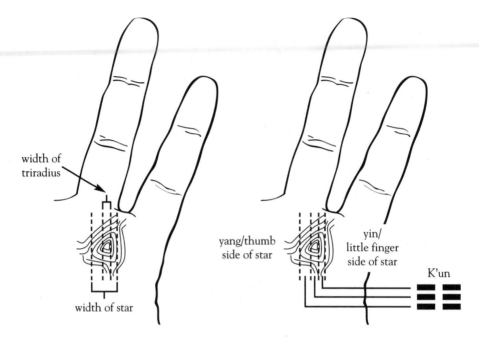

width of
triradius

yang/thumb
side of star

yin/
little finger
side of star

K'un

width of star

Figures 11.5 and 11.6—Dividing the star (left)
and determining the changing and stable lines of the trigram (right)

area's strength are a deep color, or the presence of vertical lines, which add to the relative strength regardless of the area's elevation. Also, we must take into consideration the presence of negative marks such as crosses, grilles, or crossbars, which weaken the area of the star. Basically, we're attempting to rate the star's three areas from strongest to weakest, although I find that the elevation is usually the best and simplest determination.

A similar analysis is performed on the section of the star that is nearest the thumb (yang) side of the hand. If that side of the star is the highest, the bottom line of the trigram is stable. If not, the bottom line of the trigram is changing.

Repeat for the section of the star on the yin side of the hand to determine the movement of the top line of the trigram. As the elevation moves between the yin and yang sides of the hand, this procedure provides us with the changing and stable lines necessary for proper oracular divination of the I Ching.

Construct your hexagram from the two trigrams of the stars you have just analyzed. Each line of the hexagram corresponds to one of the six I Ching interpretations. The changing lines tell you which interpretations apply.

For example, if change is in the third, then you read the interpretation corresponding to the third line from the bottom.

In my case, my Sheng hexagram came out looking like the following:

This gives me the following oracle: Change in the first line speaks of the great good fortune that results from pushing upward with confidence; change in the second line can indicate an unconventional approach, but no harm is done due to the sincerity of the intentions; and change in the top line reminds one to be conscientious and consistent, and avoid self-delusion.

As you can see, this technique opens up myriad possibilities for the hand reader. We can now use the changing energies of the hand to consult the single most powerful oracle in the world!

Let me share a story about how astonishing this technique can be. I was doing a reading for one of my regular clients, whose wife was about to make a missionary trip to South America. My client wanted to know if his wife's return trip home would be uneventful.

Using the pendulum method, I constructed a hexagram for my client and looked it up in the I Ching. The hexagram was number 54, which is called "The Marriageable Maiden." The changing lines spoke about a strong-willed woman, sexual and marital indiscretion, and a violation of proper behavior leading to disaster. As I read these paragraphs, my client's face turned whiter and whiter. "Uh oh," I thought. "He suspects that his wife is cheating on him with someone from her church."

However, the I Ching knew much more about the situation than I did. My client told me that he was being aggressively pursued by a woman who worked out at his health club, and that he was considering "getting together" with her during his wife's trip. He never mentioned this during the reading, and was somewhat taken aback that the oracle seemingly read his mind. To tell the truth, I was a bit taken aback myself, and I'm accustomed to magick happening! When working with the I Ching, I often get the feeling that it's alive.

In this case, rather than directly answering my client's question, the I Ching addressed the really important matter that was on my client's mind: whether or not he should have a fling while his wife was away! Fortunately, he took the warning to heart and didn't act on the woman's advances, thus sparing himself and his wife future misfortune.

I hope you'll find this integration of hand reading with the I Ching as fascinating as I have. The next chapter is an overview of the I Ching, which should be more than enough to get you started. Proceed carefully, and learn the technique well, and you'll find it a constant source of inspiration.

The great man changes like a tiger.
Even before he questions the oracle
He is believed.

— I Ching

chapter twelve

AN OVERVIEW
OF THE I CHING

*The fundamental idea of the I Ching can be
expressed in one single word, Resonance.*

—Chang Yeh-Yuan, *Shih Shou Hsin Yu*

This section will describe each of the sixty-four hexagrams of the I Ching.
This isn't meant to be an exhaustive discussion of the hexagrams, but just
enough to get you started. If you're interested in pursuing this branch of divination, I recommend you study some of the excellent texts mentioned in the bibliography. Good luck!

LOCATING THE HEXAGRAM

Once you've determined the two major trigrams as described earlier, use Table A
to locate the appropriate hexagram.

Next, look up the corresponding text below and see how it applies to your current situation. The "Changing Lines" sections correspond to the lines of the hexagrams from the bottom up.

UPPER TRIGRAM

	Ch'ien	Chen	K'an	Ken	K'un	Sun	Li	Tui
Ch'ien	1	34	5	26	11	9	14	43
Chen	25	51	3	27	24	42	21	17
K'an	6	40	29	4	7	59	64	47
Ken	33	62	39	52	15	53	56	31
K'un	12	16	8	23	2	20	35	45
Sun	44	32	48	18	46	57	50	28
Li	13	55	63	22	36	37	30	49
Tui	10	54	60	41	19	61	38	58

LOWER TRIGRAM

Table A

HEXAGRAM 1

Ch'ien (Heaven)

The image of Heaven over Heaven—the first hexagram—shows auspicious *beginnings*. The six yang lines represent a dragon rising from the ocean depths to the earth's surface, and from there to the sky. Therefore, success is assured. Move ahead with confidence.

Now is a great time to begin a new job, new project, or new undertaking. If you're thinking about starting a new relationship or even a family, the time is ripe. Your ambitions are within your grasp, and your goals are achievable.

Your assertive powers are at their peak. However, Ch'ien also warns against getting carried away with your own power. Don't be like the dragon who flew so high that he scorched his wings and plummeted back to the earth! Act humbly but with determination, and everything will work out for the best.

Changing Lines

First Yang: Keep a low profile and work quietly.

Second Yang: Good results if you proceed tentatively.

Third Yang: Be alert and conscientious; beware hidden dangers.

Fourth Yang: Now is a good time to take chances.

Fifth Yang: Great success!

Sixth Yang: Don't get carried away with your success, or things will go against your wishes.

HEXAGRAM 2

K'un (Success)

Consisting of twin images of Earth, K'un works with Ch'ien to make all things possible. However, unlike the aggressive yang forces of Ch'ien, K'un consists of six yin lines, suggesting a more passive approach. Like the earth for which it's named, K'un nurtures and protects, rather than forcing movement. Ch'ien *moves*; K'un *waits*. Like a strong but gentle mare, you bear your burden amiably.

Confucius likened this to walking carefully on thin ice. A light, steady step is more successful than a firm and forceful one. Therefore, be empathic, sympathetic, and reasonable in your dealings with others. Accept things as they are and don't try to change them. Cooperate with the conditions in which you find yourself.

The lesson here is that all things change of their own accord. It's important to know this and plan for the future rather than assuming that any situation is permanent. At times it will be necessary to subordinate yourself to others. Other times you'll see others rewarded ahead of you, or benefiting from your efforts while you are overlooked. Don't fret over this; just do your work steadily until conditions change.

K'un also reminds us that it's important to maintain a harmonious balance between our mind and body. Take care of yourself as well as you take care of others.

Come to terms with your body's limitations and infirmities, and make the most of what you have.

Changing Lines
First Yin: Prepare for upcoming difficulties.
Second Yin: Good results if you act with forthright honesty.
Third Yin: Be diligent; keep a low profile and follow instructions.
Fourth Yin: No rewards or advances at this time. Be patient.
Fifth Yin: Humility is required. Be courteous to those in a subordinate position.
Sixth Yin: Too much aggression, ambition, or excess causes a setback.

HEXAGRAM 3

Chun (Difficult Beginning)

The third hexagram is represented by Thunder and Water, and represents *difficulty getting started*. Sometimes Chun is seen as a blade of grass trying to grow out of the ground around a rock. Other sources describe Chun as birthing pains. Whatever metaphor is used, it signifies the necessity to plan carefully and make sure that you clearly understand the situation before acting. Good results—like a successful birth—sometimes require long periods of gestation.

Imagine that you're planning to knit a sweater, but all of your yarn is a tangled mess. Before beginning the project, you have to sort the yarn out into different skeins. Likewise, look at the apparent chaos of your situation and try to break your task down into easier, simpler portions. If possible, seek advice from others who have already accomplished what you're trying to do.

There's a danger that through a lack of preparation you'll get off on the wrong foot. Be careful what you say and do, and carefully plan your first steps. Once you get past the initial difficulties, the task will become simpler and you can walk with a bolder tread.

Even if you observe all these cautions, however, success is not assured. With Chun, there's a grave risk that things won't go as planned. Be prepared for the unexpected.

Changing Lines

First Yang: Your progress is blocked for the moment. Bide your time.

Second Yin: You're stuck in a rut, you need to ask for help.

Third Yin: You can't force things to be right; this is a situation where nobody comes out ahead.

Fourth Yin: The situation is salvageable. Now is a good time to proceed.

Fifth Yang: Fall back and conserve your resources until a more opportune moment.

Sixth Yin: Don't give up just because you've gone in the wrong direction. Fall back, choose a different approach and try again.

HEXAGRAM 4

Meng (Inexperience)

Meng is represented by a spring of Water at the foot of a Mountain. This represents the *inexperience* of the young.

We don't blame children for acting foolishly, but when they grow into adults, they have to learn to act with maturity. Likewise, we each have to consider the consequences of our actions.

In the family, we educate our children with a balance of gentleness and discipline. However, even when well treated, it's only natural for youth to rebel. This rebelliousness is the first step toward independence. A good parent will not force advice on the young, but will be available when such advice is needed.

Education is essential for maturity. However, a student must come to the teacher, not the other way around. A student must hunger for knowledge; it cannot be forced upon an unwilling person. When we're young, we think we know everything. As we mature, we learn our limits and act accordingly.

We treat the folly of the inexperienced not as something evil, but as false steps made through ignorance. A good parent, like a good teacher, corrects the inexperienced person with patience and understanding, and avoids anger. It is better to educate than criticize.

Sometimes young people will emulate a hero, and pattern their behavior after the object of their admiration. This is understandable, but success doesn't come from slavishly imitating the successful. One must grow into his or her own identity. Don't be swept away by the glamour and flashiness of those whom you admire. When you need help, find someone who is willing to instruct you. When someone you know needs help that you're qualified to give, let that person know you're there for him or her when he or she is ready.

We must also be careful to control our passions, desires, and impulses during this time. Mature people acknowledge their desires, but don't let the desire rule their life. Don't be like the young lover who loses all sense of reason and objectivity because he or she is overwhelmed by passion.

Changing Lines

First Yin: Practice self-discipline and restraint; success will follow.

Second Yang: Understand the situation thoroughly before trying to tell others what to do.

Third Yin: Don't lose yourself to greed and desire. Remember that the most important things in life can't be bought.

Fourth Yin: Study, study, study! Learn the skills you need to succeed at your endeavor.

Fifth Yin: A willingness to learn the ropes can take you far.

Sixth Yang: Don't take it out on others because you're mad or upset. It's better to explain yourself and your actions, rather than be misunderstood.

HEXAGRAM 5

Hsu (Patience)

The image is that of Water and Heaven. Rain falls from the sky to nourish the planet, but we cannot (as yet, anyway) make it rain anytime it suits us. We have to *wait* for it.

Whenever I advise one of my clients to be patient, I get a variety of responses. The most common is a rolling of the eyes with a rueful grin. I think that patience is the hardest of the virtues to master. It is hard, but sometimes you have to plod through muddy ground to get where you're going.

On the other hand, it is important not to confuse waiting with wishful think-ing. You have to cultivate an inner confidence that what you're waiting for *will* happen. You have to keep your mind on the goal and work steadily for its fruition. Even in the middle of a waiting period, you may enjoy small rewards.

If you're hoping for a change, you have a little bit longer to wait. Things are going to pretty much stay the same for a while. Just stay the course and eventually you'll receive a signal that it's time to act.

If you're in a stressful situation, it's important to let it play out to its conclu-sion. If you get angry and impatient, you'll only add to the confusion. Stand calmly and wait for things to sort themselves out. Sometimes the best thing to do is *nothing*.

Changing Lines

First Yang: I hate to have to tell you this, but be patient. There's danger ahead, so bide your time.

Second Yang: There are problems ahead, but you'll prevail as long as you face the difficulties calmly.

Third Yang: You're in a very vulnerable position. Practice extreme caution.

Fourth Yin: You have to bear up under current conditions for a while longer.

Fifth Yang: Take a rest period to refresh yourself before proceeding!

Sixth Yin: Believe it or not, what's happening right now is a blessing in disguise.

HEXAGRAM 6

Sung (Conflict)

Again, this is Heaven and Water, but they are moving in opposite directions. Thus there is *conflict*.

Sung represents a particular type of conflict—one where you know you're right, but you're blocked by opposition. The I Ching advises that you set aside your anger and think so clearly about the conflict that you can meet the opposi-tion with confidence. Hard as it may be to believe at times, conflict can actually define a path of creativity and growth.

Sometimes when we know we're in the right, we're tempted to resort to craft and guile to get our point across. However, it's vital that we don't give in to this temptation. Any attempts to manipulate other people will only make matters worse. Let the truth speak for itself. Ignore gossip, walk away from attempts to lead you into fruitless arguments, and be willing to make concessions in order to bring about a cessation of the conflict.

I've found that Sung comes up a lot when my client is concerned about the outcome of a legal matter. If this is the case, you have to be very honest with yourself. If you are to blame, it will come out and you'll be embarrassed. If you are in the right, you'll probably prevail. If you feel that you were treated unjustly, you'll have another chance to prove your innocence.

Changing Lines

First Yin: Don't worry about what other people think, say, or do. Also, don't always believe everything you're told.

Second Yang: Good results if you try to meet in the middle.

Third Yin: Making concessions and listening to the other person's needs leads to success.

Fourth Yang: You may have to swallow your pride and walk away from a fight. Don't worry; this will be in your favor.

Fifth Yang: Your cause will be heard; your complaints listened to. Justice will go to your side.

Sixth Yang: You can pursue a disagreement to the bitter end, but there will be repercussions.

HEXAGRAM 7

Shih (The Army)

Shih represents Water in the Earth—a metaphor for the power stored up in a *group*. Just as an army stores rations of water upon which to draw during battle, so does the group benefit from drawing upon the power stored within.

The power that can be generated by a group of people with a common goal is well documented. The power of group prayer, meditation, or visualization can bring into being strength far greater than the sum of the individuals' energy.

When working with a group, it is vital to keep open the lines of communication. Make sure there is strong leadership, and that everyone understands what is expected.

Also strive for realistic goals. It doesn't do any good to set a goal beyond the abilities of your group. Don't set your aspirations so high that failure will result from a lack of experience.

Practice the skills of management, leadership, and planning. Appoint tasks to people who are best qualified for the job. Learn to delegate responsibilities to competent individuals.

If you don't happen to be part of a group that can help you achieve your goal, perhaps it is time to find one. A support group, task force, or just an assembly of like-minded friends can go a long way toward making your aspiration a reality.

There's a more subtle interpretation of Shih that I've found extremely useful at times. Remember the hexagram represents Water stored in the Earth—like an earthen jug. It is possible that you are the jug and the water represents your inner resources. Sometimes this can mean that you have to work on building your inner resources—spirituality, patience, compassion, strength, determination—for a time when you'll need them to sustain you during a period of conflict.

Changing Lines
First Yin: Make sure that you're ready before you begin. Prepare well for any undertaking.
Second Yang: Communication is good, so success should follow naturally.
Third Yin: Be prepared to suffer a few setbacks.
Fourth Yin: Remain still and be careful.
Fifth Yin: Find out who is not working with you and get rid of them.
Sixth Yin: Be careful whom you trust to carry out important tasks.

HEXAGRAM 8
Pi (Holding Together)

This is the image of Water in an Earthen bowl. Pi represents *coming together*, like the various streams of water on the earth's surface that eventually flow together into a common body. Therefore, we sometimes have to sublimate our personal agenda for the sake of maintaining unity. Successful marriages, for example, place the needs of the marriage above the selfish needs of the couple. Thus, the marriage grows deeper and more satisfying.

Pi also addresses the subject of time. Don't be afraid of the future, nor have regrets about the past. Concentrate on the current situation and act with clear, honest intent. Let the past and the future take care of its own.

Sometimes it falls upon *you* to be the glue that holds everything together. In your dealings with others, be unaffected and open. You never know when you'll meet an unexpected ally. However, don't try to force yourself on others, or you'll drive them away. Just be yourself.

Changing Lines
First Yin: Honesty is the best policy here. Say what needs to be said calmly and without resentment.
Second Yin: A partnership based on honesty will flourish.
Third Yin: There's a real danger here that you're about to form an alliance with the wrong person. Watch yourself!
Fourth Yin: Expand your circle of friends and give advice sparingly.
Fifth Yang: Past failures continue to haunt you, but they have no bearing on this situation. Don't worry so much about the future.
Sixth Yin: Decisive action is needed; you're like a team without a leader.

HEXAGRAM 9
Hsiao Ch'u (Taming the Small)

Represented by a gentle Wind and Heaven, Hsiao Ch'u warns us that now is not the time for large, sweeping progression. Concentrate on *small things;* the minutiae of daily life. In other words, now is a good time to get your ducks in a row. "Duck-rowing," as my aunt used to say, "is almost a lost art." Sometimes we get swept away by the seduction of our aspirations and try to do too much too quickly.

To be proficient in any endeavor, we must first have mastered the basics. Make sure your skills are honed.

Subtle action is required here. The word *taming* is important in this hexagram's name. You can still be extremely influential, but only in a subtle, restrained way. Think of the old proverb, "An ounce of prevention is worth a pound of cure." Try to be a calming influence in a volatile situation. Practice diplomacy, empathy, and objectivity.

Another warning inherent in this hexagram is not to blow small things out of proportion. The I Ching uses as an example a quarrelsome married couple, who, instead of working together, will argue over anything. Their obstinacy prevents them from accomplishing anything. Avoid, if at all possible, this kind of behavior.

Changing Lines

First Yang: Turn back and approach the problem from a different angle. Drawing on past experience might help.

Second Yang: To be dragged away from conflict is a good thing. Don't fight it.

Third Yang: Obstinacy won't be helpful in mending tensions. Things will only get worse.

Fourth Yin: Your partnership needs to be that of equals. Mutual support will make it work.

Fifth Yang: Set a good example and you'll attract others to you.

Sixth Yang: Be careful; there's danger here. Conserve your strength for now and wait for the storm to pass.

HEXAGRAM 10
Li (Tread Carefully)

With Heaven above and the Lake below, Li warns us that the situation is difficult and to be *cautious*. Representing two extremes, this hexagram often deals with social, ethnic, and religious differences. The advice is to treat everyone equally and with understanding, and by doing so, minimize friction. Sometimes envy or distrust can arise if two people are from different socioeconomic classes. Differences in religious or political beliefs are also hazardous territory that must be approached carefully.

We may find ourselves dealing with unreasonable people during this time. Argument and debate won't help matters; now is a time to rise above the conflict and go about your business quietly. Avoid aggression, resentment, and anger, and don't let your temper lead you to say things you'll regret later.

Often we're tempted to advance ourselves to a loftier position not because we desire the position in and of itself, but because we crave escape from our lowlier circumstances. This leads to unhappiness, even if we attain the position. After the thrill of accomplishment wears off, we realize that we wanted the position for all the wrong reasons. We weren't running toward our goal, we were running away from what we saw as inferior circumstances. Without a clear vision toward which to work, our actions can become chaotic and directionless. We may attain worldly success, but our achievements will lack the spiritual component the soul needs to feel complete.

However, this situation isn't without hope. The lofty—if unsatisfying—position can provide sufficient leverage to find another position that suits you better. Live and learn . . .

Changing Lines
First Yang: Try to simplify your life and live a healthy and virtuous lifestyle.
Second Yang: It's better at this time to pull back from the mainstream and be secluded for a while. Think about what's right for *you*.

Third Yin: Don't try to act stronger than you really are. Avoid making promises you can't keep.

Fourth Yang: This is a risky situation, but if you're careful, you should come out on top.

Fifth Yang: Your situation is unstable and precarious, but you can come out all right as long as you're honest with yourself. Are you ready for this?

Sixth Yang: Stay on top of things, act responsibly, and immediately correct any mistakes you make.

HEXAGRAM 11

T'ai (Peace)

This is Earth and Heaven, each in its proper place. It also shows the perfect union of yin and yang; man working with woman as equals. Everything is in place for *success*.

The I Ching mentions that when you pull up a blade of grass, other blades come with it. This reminds us to find people whose goals and abilities complement our own and work with them. It also suggests that you'll be rewarded far beyond your efforts. You'll get more than you asked for; a bonus.

I also see this as representing an inner cooperation between our material and spiritual selves. The same rules that apply to having a satisfying relationship between man and woman can apply to the relationship between our mind and our spirit: love, respect, and communication. After all, Heaven and Earth seem far apart, but this doesn't mean that cooperation is impossible.

T'ai shows a period where everything is in balance and prosperity is more likely. You'll be paid well for your work. After all, it isn't a stress-free life that we crave; we just want adequate rewards for our efforts.

However, we mustn't become complacent just because things are going our way for the moment. In the middle of our happiness, we still have to keep an eye out for calamity. Bad luck and good luck can, after all, coexist. The I Ching is the book of *changes*, and we have to prepare for the time when our current situation gives way to another, as it inevitably will.

Changing Lines

First Yang: You'll get more than you expected. Your efforts pay off in a bigger way than you anticipated.

Second Yang: You can expect both conditions and people to cooperate with you. Take full advantage of this time of growth.

Third Yang: No situation is perfect; even though things will go your way, be aware of hidden dangers that threaten your progress.

Fourth Yin: Communication should be good between you and those around you.

Fifth Yin: You can relax and enjoy the simple pleasures and peaceful moments that T'ai brings.

Sixth Yin: Use the peaceful times to prepare yourself for the turmoil that's about to follow. Things are about to get a little turbulent.

HEXAGRAM 12

P'i (Standstill)

P'i is the opposite of T'ai, and shows Heaven and Earth in the wrong places. While the top yang line promises ultimate success, you still must go through a period of *stagnation* before attaining your goal.

You've hit a roadblock. During this period, confusion reigns. You may feel that your life is out of control; that the forces of fate are working against you. People upon whom you depend seem unreliable and unfocused. Your goals elude you and your energy is scattered over myriad tedious and insignificant matters. You just can't seem to win.

The frustrating thing is that you can *see* your goal, and you know if the minor obstacles were removed, you could easily get to it. Unfortunately, during this time, the Universe isn't cooperating. You feel like you're furiously spinning your wheels, but not making any progress.

During the period of P'i, the foolish and incompetent are rewarded while the capable and wise are ignored. The I Ching advises that you maintain your dignity and follow what your heart tells you is the correct course of action.

The good news is that, while you have to live with this impasse for the present, the blockage is by no means permanent. Conserve your energy and wait for a time when your opportunities are better. Just as the passive yin lines of the hexagram eventually turn to yang, so will your power eventually reach its zenith. Don't despair—your time is coming!

Changing Lines

First Yin: Try to distance yourself from the conflict around you. Your energy can be more wisely spent.

Second Yin: Don't be petty and insincere. Acting in a contrived manner in order to get what you want will come back to haunt you. Be honest and forthright.

Third Yin: Attempts will be made to tempt you into doing something you know you shouldn't. Resist the temptation and good results will follow.

Fourth Yang: Use this time to organize your life and work on self-understanding.

Fifth Yang: Don't give up yet—the stagnation is about to lift! Keep plugging away.

Sixth Yang: The blockage has lifted. Things are about to get a lot easier.

HEXAGRAM 13

T'ung Jen (Friends)

Consisting of Fire and Heaven, this hexagram reminds us that we're not alone. Our friends, families, and coworkers are there to help us if we let them.

We shouldn't try to accomplish tasks alone during this period. Now is the time to seek help and understanding among those whom you trust.

Unfortunately, there are sometimes people who say they're our friends when in reality they're not. We also run the risk of falling among bad companions who'll lead us away from the path of proper behavior. Be careful of your alliances and stand by your values so that everyone can see where you truly stand. Don't sacrifice what you believe in for the sake of winning friends. Your true friends love you despite any small differences in opinion or belief.

Changing Lines

First Yang: Don't be snooty or judgmental. Everyone has their place in the scheme of things.

Second Yin: Being cliquish and staying within your established circle of friends will only make matters worse. You'll miss opportunities to make new close friends and learn valuable lessons about yourself.

Third Yang: There seems to be distrust and mutual suspicion here. Step back and try to see the matter objectively. Don't share your plans with others at this time.

Fourth Yang: Don't back an unjust cause; don't attack just because you know you can win. The best action here is to protect yourself while avoiding aggression.

Fifth Yang: Your situation is at risk; the threats against you are backed by strength. Find out who's on your side and make a good defense.

Sixth Yang: You're about to be rewarded for your patience. Harmony is on its way.

HEXAGRAM 14

Ta Yu (Abundance)

Represented by Fire above Heaven, Ta Yu shows success and *abundance*. Your powers are at their height and your resources at your command. All that remains is for you to harvest the fruits of your labors. It's a time of prosperity and happiness.

Even though this is a good time for you to achieve your goals, ongoing success is maintained through modesty and unaffected living. Avoid arrogance and selfishness; be magnanimous in your dealings with others. The best way to live is simply, so even during a period of great fortune and wealth, don't let your lifestyle outgrow your capacity to maintain during slow times. Possess as though you possess nothing.

You've heard it before: "If you love something, set it free." Therefore we have to be willing to sacrifice our wealth in order to keep it. Find a good cause to support; give a portion of your abundance to your church, to the less fortunate, or to a worthy charity. Pay the Universe first, and then pay yourself. The secret of managing success is through sincerity, honesty, and generosity. They're simple concepts, but oh so easy to lose sight of.

Sometimes, sudden success can be destructive. It's almost a cliché that people who win the lottery are ruined by the sudden change of circumstances. Property, money, position—these take firm management and proper handling. Your possessions can come to own *you* as much as you think you own them.

It takes time to get used to success. Enjoy your abundance, but don't let it go to your head.

Changing Lines

First Yang: Avoid risky endeavors at this time, and your luck will increase.

Second Yang: You're ready to tackle the challenge. Go for it!

Third Yang: Be generous with your resources and use them to help others. Your reward will be multiplied tenfold.

Fourth Yang: Don't parade your accomplishments; be humble. Enjoy the fruits of your success quietly and among friends.

Fifth Yin: Humility and dignity will get you farther than pride and foolish behavior.

Sixth Yang: The Universe is on your side right now; move forward with assurance.

HEXAGRAM 15

Ch'ien (Modesty)

Ch'ien combines the Earth with the Mountain and urges us to practice *modesty*. If we maintain a humble, courteous attitude toward others, we'll be successful. By avoiding arrogance and selfishness, we'll become respected and trustworthy.

Therefore you must meet adversity and obstinate people with politeness and consideration. "You can attract more flies with honey than vinegar." When dealing with others, try to see things from their point of view. Often, anger that seems directed at you is actually about something else entirely.

To get what you want out of life, give others what they want. Show an interest in other people and they'll reciprocate. Service to others has its own rewards.

Humility is essential to a harmonious life, but modesty shouldn't be mistaken for passivity. We have to carry out our duties with determination, but we don't have to be pompous and boastful about it.

Despite great temptation to do so, try to avoid flaunting your success. It's sometimes said that "success is the best revenge," but truthfully, there's no such thing as a "best revenge." Nothing good comes from a desire for payback. Enjoy your success and happiness as a child would, with no dark agenda. You have nothing to prove to anyone.

I find that Ch'ien comes up with amazing regularity for those clients who are self-described "control freaks." The lesson here is obvious: realize that you're not responsible for the whole world and you don't always have to be the one who takes care of everything. Attempts to control others lead to conflict; attempts to control situations lead to chaos. Both will wear you out. A person can influence others in a more subtle manner by polite suggestions rather than by ordering them around.

Finally, it's important to learn to distinguish between important battles and insignificant ones. Perhaps we're determined to win a battle that has no significance except to our ego. Such battles are a waste of time and energy that could be used to accomplish a greater good.

Changing Lines
First Yin: The more honest and modest you are, the greater you'll be respected.
Second Yin: Don't be ungrateful. Count your blessings and be thankful for what you have.
Third Yang: Don't fret because your talent hasn't been recognized. Continue to work diligently—and humbly—and you'll have your day in the sun.
Fourth Yin: Don't be swept away by flattery. If it sounds too good, it probably is.
Fifth Yin: However, don't be *too* modest. Even humility can be taken too far. Don't let others walk all over you.
Sixth Yin: Modesty isn't the same as weakness or passivity. You can be firm and strong during this time. Stand up for yourself and protect your position.

HEXAGRAM 16
Yü (Enthusiasm)

Combining Thunder and Earth, overall this hexagram is a sign of *progress*. However, there are also warnings attached to it. Your enthusiasm is a terrific source of energy, but don't let it cause you to rush in to a situation and act foolishly. For example, don't be too "full of yourself" and act in a boastful or extravagant manner. The I Ching says that self-aggrandizement is a sure path to losing all that you've worked for. Also, be careful where you direct your enthusiasm. Make sure you spend it on some worthwhile endeavor, and not fritter it away on self-indulgence.

During the time of Yü, your strength of character is at its height. Therefore, now is a good time to work on correcting bad habits. Approach that exercise program, self-improvement project, or healthy lifestyle change with renewed enthusiasm.

We're also warned against playing up to the rich and powerful while ignoring the weak and humble. Playing up to those in power will only work against you. Treat everyone—the high and the low—with equal respect.

Changing Lines

First Yin: You're in a poor position to be boastful or extravagant. Be humble and watch what you say.

Second Yin: Don't be misled by the illusion of success and abundance presented by others. You must be strong and determined. Follow your heart and not your pocketbook, and you'll avoid danger.

Third Yin: Spend your time and energy helping the less fortunate. Don't suck up to the rich and powerful. Helping those less fortunate than you will come back tenfold.

Fourth Yang: Friends are important during this time. Don't alienate others through being overambitious. Treat everyone, rich or poor, with respect.

Fifth Yin: This is going to be a rough time so you must conserve your power for important things. Don't waste time and energy worrying or fretting. Look ahead and plan accordingly.

Sixth Yin: Too much indulgence can ruin you. Now is a great time to examine your habits and work on breaking the bad ones.

HEXAGRAM 17
Sui (Agreement)

Sui consists of Thunder rippling the calm surface of the Lake, an ominous sign that big changes are on the horizon. It behooves us to read the signs and *adapt* accordingly.

During this time we need to gather information. Listen to the opinions of others, even when they differ from what you want to hear. It's time to let go of old strategies and outdated attitudes as they will no longer work in the new situation. Sometimes this means that we have to end destructive relationships whose time has passed. We'll be sad at first, but ultimately we'll realize that we acted for the best.

Sui indicates a sensitive time during which you have to be careful of your actions. Choose wisely, and when the change comes, you'll be in a position to capitalize on it. It's almost certain that others will attempt to lead you into immoral action. By all means, avoid this temptation. Be flexible and alert, and you'll enjoy good results.

Changing Lines

First Yang: Hear arguments for and against your position; weigh each side impartially. Accept constructive criticism when it's well attended.

Second Yin: Your shyness may prevent you from making yourself known to people who can be helpful to you. Try to cultivate positive relationships.

Third Yin: There are bad influences around you; you must get rid of them. This will be difficult, but it's necessary. Distance yourself from those who would lead you into destructive behaviors.

Fourth Yang: Your power is strong at the moment; be careful not to abuse it. Listen carefully to those around you and act wisely. Your actions can have powerful consequences right now.

Fifth Yang: Seek out good advice from those who have achieved what you're trying to do. Don't listen to negative people; find out what you need to know and break out on your own.

Sixth Yin: You've gone about as far as you can go in this situation. Either enjoy it to the fullest or prepare yourself to make a change; you've reached the limit.

HEXAGRAM 18

Ku (Decay)

Ku is depicted by the Mountain and the Wind, and is usually pictured as a bowl full of rotting food. The situation is wrong; not by the actions of fate or karma, but by the actions of people. Something has been *ruined,* and it's up to us to fix it.

Sometimes this hexagram comes up in a family with a repeating destructive dynamic, such as alcoholism that has been passed down through the generations, or abusive tendencies that spreads throughout like dominoes falling. You have the power to let it go no further. You can redeem the family honor by repairing the damage. By healing yourself, the family heals.

Ku can also refer to a relationship that has decayed to the point that you think any attempt to fix it is hopeless. This isn't the case, however. Even though you're in a situation that's decaying, it can still be repaired. Communication and understanding can help a great deal.

In any case, the situation can be redeemed through firm, decisive action. Don't overreact, though; this can sometimes make matters worse. It takes a concerted effort over time to repair the damage.

Changing Lines

First Yin: If you're in a period of change, be on the lookout for all possible dangers. There's quite a bit of chaos around you and you must sort through it to avoid making bad decisions.

Second Yang: You'll want to help, but your assistance will be spurned. Just try to set a positive example and wait for the right time when your advice will be welcome.

Third Yang: Attack the situation with a positive attitude. Don't give up! Your minor problems and distractions will disappear and you can tackle the bigger issues with a clear mind.

Fourth Yin: Don't hold back offering advice and help, even if you're embarrassed to do so. It's better to try to help than to stand back and watch everything collapse.

Fifth Yin: It looks bad—almost hopeless—but hard work over time can fix it.

Sixth Yang: You do not always have to be the one responsible for seeing that everything gets finished. Even the king gets to retire when his work is done. You've earned your rest. Even in retirement, you can still advise others.

HEXAGRAM 19

Lin (Approach)

In this hexagram, Earth is nourished by Water, heralding the *approach* of positive change. Like the springtime, spirits are rising in anticipation of better times.

Everything is getting ready to bloom. You're about to be noticed by those in positions of influence; your prospects are about to get better, and new opportunities for growth await you.

However, just like a gardener, you have to cultivate the seeds of your success. Treat negative attitudes and habits that could hinder growth as though they were weeds. Plan for possible setbacks, make the way free for forward movement, and determine to make the most of each situation.

In relationships during this time, everything is ahead of you. There's vast potential for growth and bonding, but keep in mind that spring doesn't last forever. Be sure to plan for the autumn, when everything that has sprouted during the spring is winding down, ready to withdraw.

Changing Lines

First Yang: When working with others, don't be swayed by fashion or trends. Make sure that the people you work with are open to new ideas.

Second Yang: Follow your own heart and your friends will like you for who you are. Not everyone will agree with you or understand your decisions, but true friends will accept you anyway.

Third Yin: Be very careful; you could lose everything if you act impatiently or through overindulgence. It's not too late to make things right, but you have to be determined.

Fourth Yin: You can work with others in harmony, with a common vision. It's a good time to meet honest, sincere partners.

Fifth Yin: Now is a time of power for you. You'll be in a position to call the shots. Others will look to you for leadership and trust your decisions.

Sixth Yin: This is a time of tremendous good fortune. Keep your eye out for that special person who holds the answers you seek.

HEXAGRAM 20
Kuan (Contemplation)

Kuan combines Wind and Earth and deals with the world of concepts and *ideas*. It can be said that all great endeavors begin with a single thought: a dream, goal, or vague idea. Kuan teaches us that this idea must be clear and strong for the endeavor to succeed. My aunt Eliza would always say, "Get your mind right before you begin."

Of course, even a great idea is worth nothing without action. The dream must be made to come true, the thought expressed in deeds and the goal striven for.

Changing Lines

First Yin: Be sure that you understand the reality of the situation. Don't be naive, and don't escape into fantasizing. What are the facts?

Second Yin: Don't be hasty. Learn from others and don't make a foolish move out of ignorance.

Third Yin: Your position is weak, yet you have to make a move in one direction or another. Look at your strengths, weaknesses, and abilities honestly before comparing yourself to others.

Fourth Yin: Now is a time to be independent and self-reliant. Don't try to lean on others; develop your own inner strength and confidence. If you follow other people, you'll stray from your goals.

Fifth Yang: Be extremely careful during this time and consider carefully the consequences of your actions. Don't let a past mistake come back to bite you. Consequently, past failures don't necessarily predict future failures.

Sixth Yang: Before taking action, examine your motives. Make sure that you're not acting out of anger, resentment, or selfishness. If what you're considering will add to the common good, then proceed immediately. If you're doing it to get revenge or to gain something that you haven't earned, turn back now!

HEXAGRAM 21
Shi Ke (Biting Through)

Represented by Thunder and Fire, this hexagram deals with the idea that *strong measures* must be adopted to prevent further wrongdoing. The classical image is of a person biting through meat. Sometimes the meat is tender, but conceals sharp bones. Other times the meat is tough and sinewy, but conceals hidden treasures.

Although it is a favorable hexagram, Shi Ke tells us that a favorable outcome depends on having our hands slapped so that we don't overreach. Therefore, if you feel that you're being punished or persecuted, try to realize that this is simply karma's way of telling you to change your approach. Sometimes small setbacks (karmic lessons) work to prevent larger future misfortunes (being born into unfavorable circumstances, for example).

Changing Lines

First Yang: Consider your current difficulties as a lesson. Try to see what positive lessons you can take away from the situation. Sometimes a strong warning is necessary to prevent future mistakes, and this time can be considered such a warning.

Second Yin: Be careful; like biting into tender meat, there can be hidden bones and sharp objects in it. Proceed with caution and be alert to hidden dangers.

Third Yin: You act just in the nick of time to avoid danger. If you've done something of which to be ashamed, it's not too late to correct it.

Fourth Yang: Hidden within these difficulties is a lump of the purest gold. Proceed with determination and confidence and you'll overcome the setbacks and achieve rewards.

Fifth Yin: You have the chance to turn bad circumstances to your advantage. Try to see how you can take the obstacles that confront you and turn them into blessings.

Sixth Yang: Frustrating, isn't it? Having your options limited is difficult to deal with. However, don't further limit yourself through avoiding your responsibilities. Work hard to get your work finished and then you will have earned your freedom.

HEXAGRAM 22

Pi (Decoration)

Pi contains the trigrams for Mountain and Fire. This stresses the importance of education, culture, and *enlightenment*.

Even a plain and uninteresting life can be made more attractive through the development of inner resources. The I Ching tells us that outer beauty isn't as important as inner beauty. So many times we're swayed by a person's glamorous appearance and learn later—often to our dismay—that the person's outer beauty masks an inner dullness.

Yes, we're often judged by our appearance, but (despite the old saying) this first impression is only temporary. Without a pure and honorable soul, people soon forget about how we look. Actions and attitudes mean more than nice clothes and expensive jewelry.

I also have to think about prisoners locked away in a cell who discover the pleasures of study, reading, and art. You can imprison a person's body, but not his or her mind.

Changing Lines

First Yang: To take the easy and comfortable way is pleasurable, but you'll learn nothing. Consider doing it the old-fashioned way. It may take longer, but you'll learn more.

Second Yin: External luxuries won't help your inner needs. You can buy a house full of beautiful things and still remain unfulfilled. Concentrate on your entire being—body, soul, mind—and let go of your toys.

Third Yang: You're caught between two equally attractive possibilities. If you try for both, you'll lose both. Don't give in to temptation; do what you know is right.

Fourth Yin: Confusion results when you're tempted by riches and finery. Take time to get to know the reality behind the glitter and you'll discover the right course of action.

Fifth Yin: Simplify your lifestyle and exist humbly. Don't live beyond your means. This may make you feel a bit uncomfortable in certain circles, but your true beauty will shine through.

Sixth Yang: Simplify, simplify, simplify! Don't try to impress others with outward ostentation. Let your inner truth speak for itself. Also, don't make things more complicated than they need to be.

HEXAGRAM 23

Po (Splitting)

Po warns of a time of decay and, eventually, collapse. The situation is precarious, like lying in a bed with a rotten leg—eventually it will all come tumbling down.

If your situation is in the power of less-than-honest people, rest assured that truth will out and they will be found out. If you yourself are acting in a less-than-honest manner, rest assured that *you* will be found out!

Use this time to plan for the future and decide what you're going to do when the situation crumbles. It *could* be turned to your advantage.

Changing Lines

First Yin: The situation is very near to collapse; the rotten wood is about to splinter. Keep your thoughts and motives pure and honest.

Second Yin: During this time you have to look to yourself for the strength to free yourself from the decaying situation. No one else can help you right now; this is a task you're meant to accomplish under your own power. Be brave!

Third Yin: You must break away from bad company and seek out honest and mature people.

Fourth Yin: The situation is falling to pieces around you and you have to get out before you suffer misfortune. Don't be afraid to assert your instinct for survival.

Fifth Yin: Take it easy; the bad times are passing; the period of disintegration is drawing to a close.

Sixth Yang: All things change. Now is a good time to pick up the remains of your situation and build a new, stronger structure. You can help others rebuild their own lives too.

HEXAGRAM 24

Fu (Return)

Fu promises a return to normalcy after the period of decay. A strong person survives the bad times and enjoys the good times.

Now is a wonderful time for growth and development. All things work toward your success at this time, so move ahead with confidence.

Changing Lines

First Yang: This is a good time for travel and for generally expanding your boundaries. Don't be afraid to try something new, especially a new relationship.

Second Yin: Allow others to help you, especially those with greater wisdom and experience. Don't be shy about asking for assistance.

Third Yin: Chances are very good for a successful outcome, but proceed with caution. There are still hidden dangers left over from the period of decay.

Fourth Yin: Although you may have many friends and acquaintances who want to help you, not all of them know what they're talking about. Disregard foolish advice and listen to those with more wisdom and experience.

Fifth Yin: This is a very strong position in which to be. Be bold, confident, and assertive, but don't forget to be kindhearted and compassionate.

Sixth Yin: With success comes new responsibilities and even new, hidden dangers. Be careful of deceit and deception. New situations can enchant you for a time, but eventually your normal life will reassert itself.

HEXAGRAM 25

Wu Wang (Not False)

This hexagram, composed of Thunder and Heaven, promises great *success*. Your actions should be both natural and fair, and try to keep your aspirations within your abilities. It does little good to dream about things that can never be, but aspiring to your natural talents is well within your grasp.

Of course, what seems impossible to us now may not be at a future time. So we need to keep our options open and not exclude the *possibility* that magic can happen at any time.

Changing Lines

First Yang: Make your mind like that of a young child: innocent, pure, and full of wonder. Then success will arise naturally. It's impossible to plan everything. Sometimes you just have to let the blessing come to you.

Second Yin: Whatever you do, no matter how unimportant it may seem at this time, do it to the very best of your abilities. You may think that it doesn't matter, but you'll receive unexpected rewards.

Third Yin: Just when you think that everything is going great, something from your past rears up and endangers your success. You have to lay this troublesome ghost from the past to rest.

Fourth Yang: You won't really like this situation, but accept it because it's an essential part of your karma. Don't complain or fret; just work your way through it.

Fifth Yang: Snags in the way of your progress frustrate you because you didn't cause them. However, it's your duty to deal with the difficulties and you'll eventually be clear of them.

Sixth Yang: This line is in a position of great strength and stubbornness. Be careful, because if you blunder on without knowing what you're doing, you'll run a grave risk of losing everything for which you've worked so hard to gain.

HEXAGRAM 26

Ta Ch'u (Taming Power of the Great)

Ta Ch'u combines Heaven and the Mountain. Both wisdom and material goods—money, food, valuables—can be stored and then used for the good of many. In other words, money stored or lessons learned in the past can be used to help present situations. Likewise, we should save our present abundance against future, possibly leaner times.

Sometimes I see Ta Ch'u as representing a deferred reward. We hold back enjoying our current wealth and knowledge for the moment, accumulating it against the time when we might need it more. It requires a good measure of foresight and mature judgment to plan ahead in this manner.

Changing Lines

First Yang: Sometimes we're so inspired by our own creativity that we can't wait to rush in and get started on realizing our vision. This line warns us to slow down!

Second Yang: With the help of others, you can get a lot more work done in less time. Accelerate your progress by working with people of like mind.

Third Yang: The real test of success is if you can maintain it over time. Achieving short-term goals that contribute nothing toward long-term success may be satisfying in the short term, but really do nothing to improve your position.

Fourth Yin: Don't take unnecessary risks during this time. Plan carefully and ease your way into new responsibilities. There's a lot of confusion right now; try to clear it away a step at a time.

Fifth Yin: Boldly deal with unpleasant situations by tracking them to the source and dealing with the source of your difficulties directly. This may take time, and it will definitely take courage!

Sixth Yang: Prosperity and well-being are just a step away. You're entering a good time. Your goals are well within your reach.

HEXAGRAM 27

Yi (Nourishment)

Represented by Mountains and Thunder, Yi resembles a mouth, with the two yang lines being the lips and the yin lines forming the mouth orifice. Yi represents a time when *nourishment* is in abundance; not only food for the body, but spiritual nourishment. The spirit must be fed along with the body, and Yi tells us that this nourishment is nearby if we have the foresight to find it.

Just as a wise person knows when to quit eating, a wise person also knows when he or she has reached his or her spiritual limit. You can only absorb so much wisdom at a time. Periods of rest between growth spurts are important. You have to give yourself time to digest new knowledge, just as to fully appreciate a fine meal, you have to clear your palate between courses.

Changing Lines

First Yang: Keep a firm rein on your lust for knowledge. If you overindulge you'll use yourself up. You can only maintain your appetite for so long before you become sated. If you try to eat too much, you'll get indigestion; if you try to learn too much, you'll become overwhelmed.

Second Yin: Accept the limits of those around you. Be generous with your resources and you'll be paid back with interest.

Third Yin: You must avoid arrogance and impetuous behavior, or it will take you *much* longer to achieve your goal. You don't know everything—yet.

Fourth Yin: It's lonely to dine alone; find others who share your tastes and spend time with them. There are unexpected pleasures in sharing your knowledge with others.

Fifth Yin: Try something new; an unorthodox approach might be just the thing for your goal to succeed.

Sixth Yang: Now is a time to savor the taste of success. Move forward with strength and determination!

HEXAGRAM 28
Ta Kuo (Great Experience)

Represented by the Sun and the Marsh, Ta Kuo is strong in the middle but *weak* at the ends. Imagine a strong beam of wood that is beginning to rot at the ends.

The current situation is under a great deal of stress and is about to collapse. Yet in the middle of this stress there's a hidden, inner strength that can survive the collapse and redirect it into a better, more stable condition. Call upon all of your inner resources if you feel that everything is falling down around you; you'll survive, and eventually prosper.

Changing Lines

First Yin: You have plenty of time to prepare for the coming time of collapse; make your preparations wisely. Plan ahead!

Second Yang: Oddly—or perhaps *karmically*—enough, stress can bring out the best in us. The I Ching likens this to an old willow tree sprouting new shoots. The decay of the current situation forces you to branch out in new directions.

Third Yang: You are like a stout beam loaded to the breaking point—don't try to take on too much more or it will all collapse.

Fourth Yang: This is an excellent position; those above and beneath you will ease your burden. You can count on help when you need it.

Fifth Yang: Make absolutely sure that the tasks you undertake are worthwhile and will bear fruit. Otherwise, your strength will be depleted when you need it most in order to accomplish vital tasks.

Sixth Yin: You're out on a weak limb, so there is danger of collapse. You're overextending yourself. There are many changes facing you, but if you tackle them one by one with a calm mind, you can prevail.

HEXAGRAM 29
K'an (The Abyss)

K'an warns of difficult situations and *hidden dangers* along your path. In K'an, both trigrams are Water. Water is a very tricky element. It can be calm on the surface and roiled beneath. Rivers flow from no beginning and toward no end. Water is restless and ever moving. Some schools of thought equate water with life: an endless movement, difficult to restrain, ever flowing. The wise person doesn't fight the tide but flows along with it until the tide changes.

Changing Lines
First Yin: Beware of being swept away by charismatic but bad influences. Avoid getting in over your depth. This is a time of great risk, so be careful.

Second Yang: Your situation is tenuous at best; you're at risk and surrounded by adversity. Now is a time to tread water; don't plan on moving forward at this time. Keep a holding pattern and try not to lose ground.

Third Yin: Nothing you do now will change the outcome. If you move forward, there is danger; if you move backward, there is danger. The signs are not good for a favorable outcome. Stay right where you are and deal with the situation. Eventually, you'll have a second chance.

Fourth Yin: This is a very stressful time for all involved. By adopting a simple lifestyle, being careful with your money, and setting a good example, everyone can ride through the turbulent times.

Fifth Yang: You reach safety after struggling through the difficulty, but everyone around you is too preoccupied with his or her own worries to help you. Be grateful that you made it through safely, and don't attempt to do too much until you get your full strength back.

Sixth Yang: Your ambitions are blocked and your freedom of action constrained, like water held back behind a dam. You have to call upon your faith to see you through and wait until the obstruction lifts. Then everything will be easier for you.

HEXAGRAM 30

Li (Shining Brightly)

Li is represented by the Fire trigram repeated twice. Therefore it represents both *illumination* and *civilization*.

Controlling fire was the beginning point of man's civilization. Fire represented light, safety, and defense against the cold and the predators that stalked by night. Tribes gathered by the fire to tell stories, pray to the gods, and dance in celebration of life's gifts. Fire is *powerful*.

Changing Lines

First Yang: A controlled burn is necessary here. Don't let your enthusiasm cause you to rush in and run about haphazardly. Make sure you know what you want to accomplish and how to achieve it, step by step.

Second Yin: The warmth of the sun shines down upon you. You're about to enter a time of wonderful good fortune. Anything you plant will grow splendidly.

Third Yang: Recognize that the sun is setting and time is short. The fire is on its last embers. Don't waste your time on trivialities. There's still time to get everything finished, but time is about to run out.

Fourth Yang: You're caught between two fires; either way you turn, you'll be burned. You have to seek help from your superiors to get out of this precarious position.

Fifth Yin: The current difficulties will pass and your tears of sadness will turn to tears of joy. You may feel that you're in the bottom of a deep well, but even in the abyss you can light a candle and send the shadows fleeing.

Sixth Yin: I associate this with the fourth and fifth steps in the Twelve Steps tradition that say: "We made a searching and fearless moral inventory of ourselves," and "Admitted to God, to ourselves, and to another human being the exact nature of our wrongs." Examine yourself with the intention of cultivating your good qualities and eradicating your bad qualities. Don't be hard on yourself—don't stand in judgment of your defects of character—but recognize where there is room for improvement and act accordingly. There will be some discomfort involved, but you'll be very glad you did this!

HEXAGRAM 31
Hsien (All-Embracing)

Consisting of Marsh sitting on the Mountain, this hexagram signifies strong *partnership*. Just as the Marsh nourishes the Mountain, which in turn supports the Marsh, so do we nourish and support each other in our daily endeavors. Usually Hsien appears when something that is separated is trying to come together, and you have the power to help it.

Changing Lines

First Yin: Don't waste time and attention on trivial matters. Even if you feel that nobody appreciates your work, do it well nevertheless. You're about to be coupled with a strong creative influence that will change the course of your life.

Second Yin: Although you'll feel the urge to attempt forward progress, avoid this impulse until a better time. If you try to run ahead now, you'll stumble into an abyss. Stay where you are, and be patient.

Third Yang: Gather your energy and prepare for a sudden move forward. Don't try to go it alone if you can help it; seek out help from those around you. Plan carefully and watch for the right moment to move.

Fourth Yang: Move quickly and with great confidence; your power is at its highest and it's time to act!

Fifth Yang: Be careful at the beginning, and go faster and faster as you go along. Build momentum as you go and you'll be able to sustain it longer.

Sixth Yin: Your communication abilities are at their height right now; you have the ability to say the things that need to be said to get the ball rolling. This doesn't last long, so make use of the opportunity while it presents itself.

HEXAGRAM 32

Heng (Constancy)

Heng consists of Thunder and Wind, two forces that seem to pass quickly yet *endure* forever. Use tried-and-true methods; strategies that worked well in the past may yet still serve you well. Look to old and enduring wisdom to seek your answers for today's problems. Long-term relationships and old friends play an important role during this time.

Changing Lines

First Yin: Don't try to go too deeply into your situation too soon. Give yourself time to grow into the position. If you try to go too fast, you'll be in danger of losing all your progress.

Second Yang: Plunge ahead with confidence. All forces are aligned with your goals and dreams. Be cautious at the very beginning, but you'll soon see that you have nothing to worry about.

Third Yang: Make sure that others recognize you are trustworthy and honorable. A good reputation will help you out a great deal, so make sure that your actions speak for you.

Fourth Yang: Make sure that you're applying your effort in a wise way. It doesn't do any good to cast seed upon barren ground, so see to it that your energy is being spent in a lucrative area.

Fifth Yin: Be very, very alert. Otherwise, you'll miss a splendid opportunity for advancement. Someone wants to get to know you better.

Sixth Yin: Don't overdo things. Work hard but also plan time for rest. Otherwise, you'll become overwhelmed and burned out.

HEXAGRAM 33

Tun (Hidden)

Tun consists of Heaven and the Mountain, and tells us to hold off any sudden moves because it's time to withdraw, plan, and *contemplate*. If you're surrounded by violence, corruption, or conflict at this time, it's better to withdraw and wait for it to pass rather than leap into the fray. Avoid being led into any action you'll regret later.

Changing Lines

First Yin: Don't procrastinate in taking care of unfinished business. Tie up all loose ends; otherwise, you'll not have the freedom of action to take advantage of a great opportunity that's just around the corner.

Second Yin: Follow a good and courageous leader. If you have a mentor or role model (an ideal person whom you try to emulate), ask him or her for advice. If you cannot ask the person directly, ask yourself, "What would _____ do?"

Third Yang: Something or someone is not what it seems to be. There's deception going on around you; beware, for you're being tricked. Try to keep a low profile and not arouse the resentment of others.

Fourth Yang: Be very careful what you say, and whom you say it to. Know when to speak and when to withhold comment. Your words can come back to bite you if you're not discreet.

Fifth Yang: You've worked hard and deserve a comfortable life. Take time to appreciate the rewards of your effort.

Sixth Yang: Don't worry; you're in a great position. Anyone who tries to stand in your way won't succeed, so don't worry about them. You're in it for the long run. Don't fret over minor annoyances and setbacks.

HEXAGRAM 34

Ta Chuang (Great Power)

Like the previous hexagram, Ta Chuang combines Thunder and Heaven, but in reverse order. Therefore, the omens are better for you, as your weaknesses take the background and your *strong leadership* power appears. We're cautioned not to allow our authority go to our head, though, and to use our newfound position of power carefully.

Changing Lines

First Yang: You'll want to show off your newfound strength (and justifiably so), but don't be surprised if nobody notices. Although your strength is apparent, now isn't the time for it to be recognized.

Second Yang: Your strength is apparent to all, and you'll be noticed. No need to overdo it though; remain modest and conservative in your displays of strength.

Third Yang: Don't be stubborn or arrogant. The I Ching compares this approach to a goat butting his head against the gate: although he is the most powerful animal in his herd, his arrogance and stubbornness make it easy to trap him.

Fourth Yang: Your stubbornness serves you well at this time. You may appear weak to others, but your inner strength will cause you to prevail.

Fifth Yin: Don't charge blindly ahead like an angry ram. You're on precarious ground. One thoughtless action at this time could cost you everything you've gained.

Sixth Yin: Approach challenges calmly. Don't be like the goat that tangles his horns in the hedges and can't move forward or backward. If you try to be forceful, you'll only end up in a deadlock. Remain flexible and keep your options open for now.

HEXAGRAM 35
Chin (Advance)

This hexagram, with its image of the Sun rising above the Earth, shows *progress*. The image is of a king who rewards his servant with several horses, and in return, the servant works even harder. This wins even more approval from the king and leads to even greater rewards. It's a win-win situation.

Sometimes when we embark on important personal work, such as pursuing our life's dream, we encounter disappointments and setbacks. We also encounter people who tell us that our dreams and goals are unrealistic and unattainable. The advice of the I Ching is to meet these obstacles and these negative people with a calm, cheerful attitude. In other words, don't argue, be pleasant, and continue on with your work in good cheer. Anger solves nothing and can actually be quite harmful. Often, people who tell you that you're wasting your time are only trying to be helpful, but that doesn't necessarily mean they're right.

Sometimes this hexagram comes up when we don't have the slightest idea what our work *is*. In this case, we should keep an open mind and wait for illumination to come to us. Like the sun rising above the earth, illumination dispels the mists.

Often, our work is done with the help of others. It's important to communicate with other people and determine where our strengths and weaknesses overlap, and what interests we may have in common. In this way, our progress is accelerated.

Changing Lines

First Yin: Don't worry if you feel that your efforts are going unrewarded. There's a bigger picture ahead that you don't yet see clearly.

Second Yin: Progress is halted for the moment. Prepare for a time where you may not see a lot of progress. Work diligently and things will begin moving again.

Third Yin: You're gradually making progress. Although you still have opposition, you won't have to worry about it because others will step in to help you. Keep your eye on the brass ring!

Fourth Yang: You'll be tempted to do something you know very well that you shouldn't. Don't give into this temptation, no matter how attractive it appears. If you do, your transgression will be found out and you'll be humiliated.

Fifth Yin: Things are definitely getting better. Your work and efforts are beginning to pay off. Congratulations!

Sixth Yang: Problems are unavoidable, but you can work around them as long as you don't become discouraged. Things are not as complicated as they may appear at first glance.

HEXAGRAM 36

Ming I (Wounded Light)

Ming I is represented by the Earth blocking the Sun, implying the coming of darkness. With darkness comes *danger*, so it's wise to move carefully. Like walking about in a dark room, take careful steps; or when in doubt, just stand still until you regain your bearings. When lost in dark woods, it's better to stay put and wait for sunrise before trying to find your way out.

It's important not to be swept up in the events around you. The light is still there, in all its clarity and purity, it's just hidden for the moment. Be patient and remain true to your vision, act as you know you should, and conditions will improve. Now is the time to practice restraint, even to the point of "hiding your light under the bushel." Lay low for a while; keep your plans to yourself.

I've often found that this hexagram warns that things will get worse before they get better. But the good news is that things *will* get better, if one is brave and patient.

Changing Lines

First Yang: Luck is not on your side right now. Stay away from temptation even if you have to sacrifice progress for your beliefs. Be true to yourself during this time.

Second Yin: This is an important time for you to examine your situation and see if you can sort through your difficulties. Ask yourself how many of your problems are under your control, and how many of them you just have to accept for the present.

Third Yang: Make your plans in secret and be careful whom you trust. You can't help it if others are less than honest, so stick to your principles.

Fourth Yin: The situation can't be fixed. There's nothing left for you to do but get as far away from it as possible. Get on with the rest of your life and don't look back.

Fifth Yin: You may have to work beneath your abilities at this time. Sometimes you have to hide your abilities to survive current difficulties.

Sixth Yin: The I Ching says that if you lack the brains to maintain your position (or as my aunt Eliza liked to say, "Can't tell the difference between cheese and Wednesday"), you'll soon lose it. If this applies to someone above you who's causing you problems, don't worry—that person will soon lose his or her position of power. If it applies to you, you must recognize that the position doesn't suit you and that you'll have to take a lower position soon.

HEXAGRAM 37
Chia Jen (Family)

The image is Wind and Fire, which represents the difference between the wildness and freedom of the outdoors and the security and warmth of the *family*. Chia Jen reminds us that it's important to understand our place in the scheme of things, and not to run away from responsibilities. It's also important not to step outside the boundaries of our place and try to take on responsibility for things that don't concern us. In other words, do your job and let others do theirs. Be firm when you need to be firm; be compassionate and flexible when this need arises.

In the family, it's important that each member contributes according to his or her role within the family unit. Likewise, each of us has a responsibility to contribute to the world in our special, unique way. We have to find our unique role and manifest it.

Sometimes we're torn between the need for the security of the home and the wildness of freedom and independence. It's important to strike a balance between these two often-conflicting needs. Take care of your responsibilities, but don't let your responsibilities become an excuse for avoiding taking chances that might lead to greater rewards.

Changing Lines

First Yang: Make sure that everyone understands the rules from the outset so that there won't be conflict in the future. Spell out your expectations clearly.

Second Yin: It's important to delegate tasks and make sure that everyone is doing his or her share. Don't tolerate those who shirk their responsibilities.

Third Yang: You have to find a balance between gentleness and severity. Be compassionate, yet firm when the situation requires it. It's nothing personal, so don't blow it out of proportion!

Fourth Yin: There's not much to say here except that you can expect a very fortunate outcome.

Fifth Yang: If you happen to find yourself in charge, treat others with the same respect and gentility as you would your own family.

Sixth Yang: By setting a good example, you inspire others to follow your lead; a fortunate outcome for everyone.

HEXAGRAM 38

K'uei (Opposition)

The image is of Fire and the Lake—opposing forces that nevertheless work together in nourishing the earth. Likewise, even though your present circumstances may seem contrary to your wishes, it's going to turn out for the *higher good*. When people are in conflict, it's difficult to achieve fast results because everyone is acting according to his or her own agenda. Therefore, small results should be sought that, over time, build to a larger result. Don't try for great strides; slow and steady wins this race.

When working with other people, it's important to overlook your differences of opinions and seek out common interests. Ask yourself, "How can we work together for the common goal?" Often, the disharmony you think you see in the situation actually brings about a stronger unity. The people who annoy you the most may become close friends.

Opposition can, at times, bring out the best in us. We stretch beyond our boundaries and achieve levels of performance that may surprise us!

Changing Lines

First Yang: There are times when the course of your life won't run smoothly. This is one of them. Don't worry; these setbacks will soon pass and be just a vague memory.

Second Yang: Don't be afraid to test your limits by accepting new challenges. You may surprise yourself with reserves of ingenuity you didn't know you possessed.

Third Yin: Elements that have been scattered come together. Although there is confusion at the beginning, it sorts itself out over time.

Fourth Yang: You may feel alone and that nobody understands you. However, an association with a more experienced person will prove you wrong.

Fifth Yin: There's no cause for alarm. You'll gain a trustworthy partner and do great work together.

Sixth Yang: Most of the things about which you are anxious are just phantoms—they're never going to happen. Calm your fears and face your difficulties with a clear mind. Fear can make you act foolishly, but if you examine your fears objectively, they can help you learn your limits.

HEXAGRAM 39

Chien (Obstruction)

This hexagram represents a Mountain behind and a Chasm ahead. In other words, your path is *blocked*; you can go no farther. The advice here is to retreat until you gain more experience in dealing with the situation; pause, reflect, and regroup. You can try again later.

Sometimes the hardest thing in the world is to admit to ourselves that we're not ready for a particular undertaking. The problem here is that if we insist on trying to confront the obstruction, we'll make mistakes and bring about disaster through our own ignorance and lack of experience. This isn't the time to try and force change.

We shouldn't give in to the temptation to blame others for this impediment to our progress. This situation, its cause, as well as its solution, is entirely our own responsibility. One possible solution, suggested by the I Ching, is to find an experienced guide to help us steer past the obstacles.

If a hostile person causes the obstruction, it's better to simply walk away than to attempt confrontation. It isn't a question of bravery; it's one of timing. This isn't the time for aggression.

Changing Lines

First Yin: The way ahead is blocked. Only by going back and starting over can you get ahead in this situation.

Second Yin: Don't take on a risky challenge just because you feel you have to. Examine your motives: are you doing this because you want to, or because you feel it's expected of you?

Third Yang: You can come out victorious as long as you don't take unnecessary risks. Know what's required before jumping in.

Fourth Yin: Don't try to go it alone right now. Get some help and then confront the challenge.

Fifth Yang: There's tremendous difficulty standing in your way, but you have friends who help you through it. Don't be afraid to ask them for help.

Sixth Yin: If you keep going like you are now, your problems will increase. Ask a wiser person to advise you.

HEXAGRAM 40

Hsieh (Release)

Consisting of Thunder over Water, Hsieh promises *release* from danger and escape from difficulties. The image of Thunder tells us that the dangerous situation is still there, but that an avenue of escape is opening up.

If your situation is cloudy, uncertain, and confusing, you can rely on the clouds dissipating to allow clarity and understanding to shine through. I often see Hsieh come up when a person is overwhelmed with responsibilities and can't decide where to turn or what to do. Usually, after examining the situation from an objective point of view, all that's really required is to determine a set of priorities. Once we know what we need to do first, the rest of the tasks naturally follow.

We can also expect a release from tension, so your situation is about to get easier. Enjoy it!

Changing Lines

First Yin: The worst is behind you; this is a time to rest, recuperate, and enjoy some quiet time. It's a good time to see new places or relearn an old interest that you used to enjoy in the past.

Second Yang: You'll have the time and the energy to take on new tasks and responsibilities and carry them to a successful conclusion. If there's a major task you've been waiting for the right time to start, this is the time!

Third Yin: Don't flaunt your success, your knowledge, or your superior position. You'll attract resentful people who will tear down what you have accomplished. Pride goes before a downfall!

Fourth Yang: You'll have the time and, more importantly, the fresh perspective to rid yourself of bad habits. It's a great time to begin a self-help program.

Fifth Yin: Be careful whom you listen to. Don't believe flattery, and if you suspect someone is just telling you what you want to hear, get another, more objective opinion.

Sixth Yin: You'll get what you're aiming for. Signs are good for success.

HEXAGRAM 41
Sun (Decrease)

Sun combines the Marsh and the Mountain. Just as we have periods of increase, so we'll have times of *decrease*. The *Tao Te Ching* says, "High winds can't blow all morning, nor can a storm rage all day." We have to plan and save up for lean times.

One thing I learned from working with contract laborers is that you don't build up your lifestyle so much during your fat times that you can't maintain it during your lean times. It's best to live comfortably within your means than to try to maintain an affluent lifestyle that you may not always be able to afford.

Changing Lines

First Yang: Complete your own work and then help others with theirs. Share your resources, but practice moderation. Don't let your generosity run away with you.

Second Yang: Be satisfied and grateful for what you have. Don't expect any more nor settle for any less. Be careful when you offer help to others; your offer may be taken the wrong way.

Third Yin: Many authorities agree that this line concerns itself with jealousy and love. Two people make a good partnership, but a third party arouses jealousy. If you're in a relationship, you may be tempted to stray. If you happen to be single, this line is a good indication that you'll find your soul mate.

Fourth Yin: You'll have to swallow your pride and ask others for help. You may find that you have to seek help from the last person you want to be indebted to. Chalk it up to karma.

Fifth Yin: Sometimes you may feel that you don't deserve praise and reward. The fact is that you do deserve the rewards of your efforts. Have faith in yourself and enjoy your successes.

Sixth Yang: This line promises increase, not decrease. You'll attract able helpers and friends, and improve your financial situation through hard work.

HEXAGRAM 42

I (Increase)

Consisting of Thunder and Wind, I promises that after a period of humble living and rationing of resources, you can count on a period of *increase*. It may be time to make that major purchase, like a car, house, or recreational vehicle, or to take on increased responsibilities in order to improve your financial situation.

I also reminds us about the importance of giving our time and energy to others. When we're enjoying times of affluence, we must remember to give over a portion of our wealth to the less fortunate. Such actions fall under the category of good karma, not only for you but also for everyone involved.

Changing Lines

First Yang: This is a wonderful time for you; you have the time, energy, and opportunity to achieve great things. Follow your dream and be true to your vision and success will eventually follow.

Second Yin: Examine your motives to make sure they're worthy of you. If you act properly and do what you know is right, you'll be even more fortunate than you hoped.

Third Yin: For the time being, keep to the middle path. Don't try to forge ahead, nor attempt to fall back. Stay right where you are and use your common sense.

Fourth Yin: There is a dispute, but a good mediator can help settle it.

Fifth Yang: To help another is to help yourself. Look for opportunities to give a helping hand to others.

Sixth Yang: Don't try to increase too much. In other words, try to avoid gaining too much too soon. Don't insist on having everything immediately; give it time.

HEXAGRAM 43

Kuai (Breakthrough)

Consisting of Marsh and Mountain, Kuai promises that the power of the weak and corrupt is about to be replaced by the strong and righteous. In terms of your life, it's time to move on to a better phase of your existence, even if it means leaving something behind to which you're attached but has long outlived its usefulness. Prepare to carve out a new path, fork off on a new direction, or be confronted with new challenges.

Changing Lines

First Yang: Imagine a very young and energetic person who approaches a challenge with great confidence, but who lacks the experience to bring about a successful conclusion. This line warns you not to behave in this manner, but take your time and seek out information before you rush off to tackle the world.

Second Yang: If you've done all you can to be prepared for this difficult time, you'll do well. Go over your plans and make sure you covered all the contingencies.

Third Yang: Don't anger those who oppose you; you must use all your diplomatic skills to ease the tensions.

Fourth Yang: Try not to be obstinate or single-minded. If you insist on having things your own way, you'll attract a great deal of opposition. If someone offers you advice, don't interpret it as an attack or as criticism, but as a helpful suggestion.

Fifth Yang: Stick to your guns; you're in the right concerning this matter. Don't let anyone sweet-talk you out of what you know is the right course of action.

Sixth Yin: The bad times are almost over. Express your desires; tell people what you expect from them. Ask the Universe for a favor. You will be rewarded!

HEXAGRAM **44**

Kuo (Meeting)

Kuo consists of Heaven and Wind. This hexagram is associated with *temptation,* and warns us to examine our motives very carefully. Often we're tempted by what we think is a more attractive possibility. The I Ching warns us that what at first appears more attractive may actually be less desirable once we understand its nature. In relationships, a third party can cause trouble. Don't throw away a good thing over a temporary thrill.

Changing Lines

First Yin: Keep your feelings under control so that you'll choose wisely. The I Ching compares this situation to a woman who is wooed by five admirers and who modestly chooses one for her husband. Likewise, don't be carried away by flattery and attention but make the best possible choice.

Second Yang: Be alert; someone else is after the prize you seek and has a head start.

Third Yang: Although your options are extremely limited right now, there's little danger in your present situation. You'll avoid making bad mistakes as long as you don't get greedy!

Fourth Yang: Don't treat others badly in your quest for success. Someday you may need to ask them for help and they'll remember how you treated them.

Fifth Yang: No need to flaunt your talents—they've already been noticed. Let things occur naturally.

Sixth Yang: You're at a standoff, neither advancing nor retreating. You may have to revise your goals before you go any further.

HEXAGRAM 45
Ts'ui (Collecting)

Marsh and Earth come together in Ts'ui to show the power of *cooperation.* This is a great time to work with others toward a mutually beneficial goal. In relationships, Ts'ui reminds us that we have to give and take in order to have a harmonious life. If we give too much, we become exhausted; if we take too much, we drive the other person away. Ts'ui is a good time to form lasting relationships and strong social groups.

Changing Lines

First Yin: Although the signs point toward your success, there are still complications. Look to an older, wiser head to help you through them. Without a clear plan, everything will fall apart.

Second Yin: Everything looks pretty good for you right now. You have the energy and skills to move ahead. Fortune favors you, so you'll reap far more than you sow.

Third Yin: This line indicates that you've tried very hard to do the right thing but are becoming discouraged. Don't give up yet though. Share your concerns with someone else and your situation will make more sense to you. You lose some things but gain others, so it balances out in the end.

Fourth Yang: People work intelligently and bring about good work. You can be a part of this if you want to be.

Fifth Yang: A strong leader is needed, and then the work will be done. If you act with efficiency, everything will turn to your advantage.

Sixth Yin: Sometimes up, sometimes down—this is the nature of life. Go with the flow and don't fight the inevitable.

HEXAGRAM 46
Sheng (Rising)

Sheng combines Earth and Wind, showing that everything is on the rise. This is an indication that you're about to enter a period of *prosperity* and promotion. Your life is growing and blooming in all directions. Unfortunately, this period of prosperity will attract a few undesirable characters who will want to ride on your coattails. Be careful whom you trust, and don't let your success go to your head.

Changing Lines

First Yin: Nothing bad here; you'll thrive and grow in a natural manner.

Second Yang: Proceed by degrees; take one step at a time and enjoy the trip!

Third Yang: No obstacles in your path at all; "You walk through an empty realm."

Fourth Yin: You can't go further because that position is already occupied. You have to wait your turn.

Fifth Yin: Step by step you advance, helping others along the way. Keep your mind calm and cheerful.

Sixth Yin: Stay the course and don't let success go to your head. Don't rest on your laurels. Keep moving forward!

HEXAGRAM 47
K'un (Oppression)

During the period ruled by K'un you may feel dispirited, cut off, *exhausted*. Consisting of Water and Marsh, it may seem as though you're plodding through mud toward an uncertain future. There is an answer: you must search your own character and determine how much of your situation is of your own making. How much baggage are you carrying? Isn't it time to let some of it go? Through proper communication, can you make the going less burdensome? Is it possible to get help and guidance? Even though the going's hard, through personal courage and self-examination, it is possible to find the most direct path through your difficulties.

Changing Lines

First Yin: You're going to struggle for a while yet before your situation begins to make more sense; be determined and steadfast. You'll greatly improve yourself and learn valuable new skills, but it might be a while before anyone recognizes this.

Second Yang: There are reasons to be optimistic because your difficulties are beginning to lessen. Light, at last, at the end of the tunnel!

Third Yin: This will be a time of loss. You'll feel restless and indecisive, but you'll just have to tolerate this state for a while. With every loss there's usually a gain.

Fourth Yang: You need the assistance of someone in a position to help you sort through your difficulties; consult an expert.

Fifth Yang: You will make progress, but slowly. Proceed cautiously, step by step. You'll ask for help but have trouble finding anyone to depend on. It's your karma that you must do this all by yourself, but your determination sees you through it.

Sixth Yin: There are so many complications and hidden traps that no matter what direction you move in, you could become ensnared. Yet if you stay where you are, nothing gets resolved. This is the result of karma: something you did in the past has led to this situation. Pause, reflect, and see what you can do to avoid repeating the past unskillful action. Then you can proceed.

HEXAGRAM 48
Ching (The Well)

Ching, the Well, is the immutable source of all things. Call it what you will—Spirit, Heaven, fate, karma—everything rises from the Well and returns to It.

Consisting of the trigrams for Water and Air, the Well can be seen as representing universal *truths*. All creatures drink from the well; cities and civilizations are built around it. Yet even the oldest well can become tainted, at which point a wise person seeks another, fresher source from which to drink.

Changing Lines

First Yin: The water is bad. It's time to give up something that no longer serves a useful purpose. Your situation has stagnated. Move on to a fresher, more satisfying source.

Second Yang: The water is muddy, so now isn't the best time to begin a new undertaking. There are too many loose ends right now. It would be like trying to plug the leaks in a collapsing dam; the tasks would overwhelm you.

Third Yang: False accusations can tarnish your reputation as much as true ones, just like you're hesitant to drink from a once-polluted well even though everyone assures you that the water has been cleaned. Be careful not to give any cause for your reputation to become soiled. Act from a clear conscience and you won't have anything to worry about.

Fourth Yin: You probably feel trapped and that you have little room to maneuver in. Behave as though everything were perfect; don't make waves if you can possibly avoid it.

Fifth Yang: The water is clear and cool. People drink from your knowledge and you're inspired by the Source. Great things can happen!

Sixth Yin: Your life is blessed by wise decisions and the well is full. You're in a position to give yourself to the world without fear of being used up.

HEXAGRAM 49

Ko (Revolution)

Ko consists of Marsh and Fire, two elements that, if out of control, can destroy each other. Ko tells us that, no matter how comfortable we may be with the current situation, to expect *radical change*.

Change is inevitable, but we tend to resist it. Often we cling to an adequate situation because we're comfortable with it. We're afraid to reach for a better situation for fear of losing our comfortable spot. But Ko tells us that we should be ready to leave our comfort zone and expect big changes. We can't control the changing nature of reality, but wisdom consists of knowing how to react during the changes.

Changing Lines

First Yang: You have a good chance of finally being noticed if you're willing to work hard. Don't expect overnight success, but you could well be on your way to achieving your goal.

Second Yin: This is the time to move fast. Take appropriate action immediately.

Third Yang: Don't think twice, think *three* times before acting; be careful.

Fourth Yang: Move with confidence and determination; try to follow a strong leader. Learn from those who have gone before you.

Fifth Yang: Great changes are afoot; be alert to opportunities to capitalize on the revolution.

Sixth Yin: Don't expect immediate reward, but adapt yourself to changing circumstances and establish good habits. Old strategies won't work anymore; you have to develop new ones appropriate to the changing situation. You'll get your reward shortly!

HEXAGRAM 50
Ting (The Cauldron)

Ting is composed of the trigrams Wind and Fire, and represents the *preparation* of a meal. To prepare a meal you must first boil the meat in the Cauldron, plan for guests, summon the guests, and serve the meal. Then you benefit from their company and take great enjoyment in their praise for work well done.

Of course, we're not literally talking about preparing food, but preparing ourselves for any task. In this manner you begin laying the groundwork for new and exciting goals. You must proceed step by step, like following a recipe: plan ahead, and know how many people will need to be "fed." When you follow the recipe correctly, everyone enjoys the meal.

Changing Lines

First Yin: In order to clean a soiled pot, you have to empty it first. In this way, empty yourself of old and outmoded habits so that you can cleanse your spirit for the new tasks ahead.

Second Yang: Keep on improving and moving ahead, although some of your associates will become jealous. Don't do anything that will leave yourself open to criticism.

Third Yang: If you cook a piece of meat in a pot without handles, you won't be able to remove the meat from the fire. However, you learned how *not* to cook a piece of meat! Sometimes the best way to learn is from our mistakes.

Fourth Yang: You have to be careful whom you trust. Just like a careless cook who overturns the pot and spills the food, so can someone carelessly overturn your life if you trust that person with more than he or she is competent enough to handle.

Fifth Yin: The cooking pot is in great shape with new handles and a shiny surface. This is a good time to complete your work. You have all the tools you need for your success.

Sixth Yang: Like the handles of the pot, you have a very important purpose. You must be pure and honest as you proceed about your business.

HEXAGRAM 51

Chen (Shock)

Containing a double image of Thunder, Chen denotes great power causing tremendous *movement*. Just as thunder rolls across the sky, Chen moves into our lives and changes everything with a single clap.

Usually Chen means that we're about to experience a time of fear or shock. Something for which we are totally unprepared is about to happen, coming—just like thunder—out of the blue. It's time to prepare for the unexpected. Often, this shock is an unexpected blessing in disguise, because it forces us to reevaluate our life and continue our forward progress. Sometime we have to be shocked into action.

Changing Lines

First Yang: Prepare to be surprised; you won't quite know how to deal with it. However, from this shock you'll learn to deal with similar situations in the future.

Second Yin: Due to unexpected circumstances, you may experience some sort of loss, but don't fret over it. Whatever you lose will return to you in time.

Third Yin: Something frightening is on the horizon, but it won't harm you. You'll face your fear and afterward you'll wonder what all the fuss was about.

Fourth Yang: The shock may be so great that you'll be unable to decide what to do, but you must snap out of paralysis and keep moving.

Fifth Yin: There's danger, but if you prepare for it, you'll emerge safely. Consider this a warning to stay alert.

Sixth Yin: The thunder grumbles; you'll hear it and know that it's time to retreat to safety. However, don't be so focused on your own safety that you forget about others who may be in the same danger.

HEXAGRAM 52
Ken (Resting)

Ken is a double image of the Mountain, and signifies repose, solidity, and *keeping still*. Just like the mountain, which supports trees, flowers, wildlife, and running streams without getting involved in any of it, so must you remain steadfast, solid, and true to your nature. Don't be distracted by what other people think, do, or say. Act according to your nature and ignore distractions.

Changing Lines

First Yin: When you begin a new phase of your life, do as much as you can in the time you're given. Build solid foundations so that you may take your ease later. Nip bad habits in the bud before they can even begin to gain a foothold.

Second Yin: Your efforts, no matter how inconsequential they may seem, are essential. Don't stop now—a lot is depending on you.

Third Yang: You may feel a bit anxious for a short time since your desires will be unfulfilled. Don't worry; the anxiety will soon pass.

Fourth Yin: It's time to rest from your efforts. Take a break and return to your tasks with a refreshed spirit.

Fifth Yin: Don't let anyone else know about your uncertainties or suspicions. This is a time to keep a close watch on what you say and do. Keep wearing your best "poker face."

Sixth Yang: Be aware that you've about reached your limits; don't overdo it.

HEXAGRAM 53
Chien (Slow Development)

The Mountain and the Wind join together to form this symbol of *gradual progress*. Just as a tree must put down strong roots so that it can resist the wind, so must a person have a deep understanding of his or her nature before undertaking a serious commitment. Progress is gradual and fortune doesn't come at a stroke. It takes time to master yourself and your craft. Give yourself time and room in which to grow.

Changing Lines

First Yin: Take things step by step and you'll be all right in the end. Be satisfied with making slow but steady progress. Celebrate each successful step forward and don't ask for too much.

Second Yin: Don't let your desire for fame and fortune make you greedy. Don't take unnecessary risks at this time.

Third Yang: Do your work carefully and diligently. Learn from the example of those who have mastered your craft.

Fourth Yin: The more responsibilities you take on, the greater the chance for error. Don't feel like you always have to be the one responsible for everything—delegate!

Fifth Yang: You have a good grasp of the situation, but someone's trying to mislead you. Whether this is deliberate or not isn't important. Ask yourself, "Do they really know what they're talking about?"

Sixth Yang: Approach the problems of each day one by one, in the proper order. If you do this, your problems will disappear sooner than you think.

HEXAGRAM 54

Kuei Mei (The Marriageable Maiden)

This hexagram represents the marriage of Marsh and Thunder, and reminds us of the importance of understanding our *proper place*. Of course, "our place" changes over time, and part of attaining wisdom is knowing when to move on to a different position. For example, we stay single for a period of time and learn about our potential soul mates. Then, when the time is right, we marry. However, we must be sure that we're suited for the position we desire or, like a marriage that gets off on the wrong foot, we'll repent our decision for a long, long time.

Changing Lines

First Yang: You're in a position beneath your abilities. It's time to move to the next level. Fight for your chance to prove yourself.

Second Yang: Your present circumstances aren't what you wish, but don't lose heart. Persevere and you'll get your break.

Third Yin: You're in a position that's beneath your usual standards. Don't settle for less than you deserve. You may need an objective point of view concerning your abilities. Ask yourself: "Am I selling myself short?"

Fourth Yang: If you're postponing a move or advancement, examine your motives. Is there a good reason to wait or are you simply afraid that you're getting in over your head? You have as much right to advance as anybody; take the chance.

Fifth Yin: While it's true that people too often judge from appearance, it's your character that will win others over for the long haul.

Sixth Yin: There's nothing to gain from deception. Be honest and truthful, even when it's difficult to do so. You'll be glad you did.

HEXAGRAM 55

Feng (Prosperity)

Feng combines Fire and Thunder, two very powerful elements, into a symbol that everything is approaching a peak or *climax*. All your efforts are about to be rewarded; all your suffering and self-denial will be recognized. Your fame arrives like thunder and your success burns like fire. The situation grows until it builds to a head, and you're riding the crest. Prepare yourself for the ending of one phase and the beginning of another.

Changing Lines

First Yang: You'll be recognized as an equal by those in a superior position, but don't let this go to your head. Be polite, courteous, and humble. Avoid a vengeful attitude that will prevent you from enjoying your good fortune.

Second Yin: Lay your cards on the table and include others in your plans. Don't try to hide your true intentions or you'll be viewed with suspicion. You may gain strong supporters through being totally open.

Third Yang: Things are looking good for you, although you still aren't able to see the big picture. Get more information before you go much further. Let the other person make the first move.

Fourth Yang: You can benefit from an objective opinion because you're too close to the issue to see it clearly. Seek out advice and perspective from a more experienced person.

Fifth Yin: Normally, you would be in a weak position, but there are people helping you—even some people of whom you're unaware. Accept help from competent people.

Sixth Yin: Don't flaunt your success or overindulge, because even times of prosperity must give way to change. Use your affluence to prepare for a rainy day.

HEXAGRAM 56
Lü (The Traveler)

Combining the Mountain and Fire, Lü tells us that it's time to move on. We have to give up complacency and stubbornness and *travel* to another place.

Lü doesn't necessarily mean that it's time to *physically* move, although it seems to come up a lot when people ask me about seeking their fortune someplace else. Often Lü suggests that we move from one attitude to another, or take a spiritual journey or a vision quest. Basically, we've become content and complacent and have lost our senses of discovery and curiosity. It's time to bring to end one phase of our life and begin a new one.

Changing Lines

First Yin: When in a strange town, a wise traveler observes the local customs and adjusts his or her actions accordingly. When you find yourself in a new situation, do the same. Observe and learn the lay of the land.

Second Yin: Before going on a journey, a wise traveler makes sure that he or she has sufficient funds and a trustworthy companion. Before you embark on a new enterprise, make sure that you have good help and sufficient resources to get at least a good start.

Third Yang: Don't make things harder for yourself by being stubborn or argumentative. Be agreeable and respectful, like a good guest.

Fourth Yang: Be thankful for whatever you're given, even if it isn't what you expected. A weary traveler is glad to have a roof over his or her head, even if it's only a barn.

Fifth Yin: A traveler is often treated with suspicion until he or she proves trustworthy. Learn to get along with those you have to work with and observe how people like to do things. Let your character guide your actions. Soon, you'll be accepted as one of the group.

Sixth Yang: Don't gloat over another's bad luck. This is not only unskillful, but when the same thing happens to you nobody will feel inclined to help you. Remember that you're the guest, not the host.

HEXAGRAM 57

Sun (Yielding)

Sun consists of two Wind trigrams. Like the wind, this hexagram tells you that you're in a weak position and have to *conform* to circumstances. The wind is mobile, restless, and unsettled; it penetrates every corner but doesn't get anywhere unless directed. Your restless energy must be directed by good leadership, otherwise your energy will be expended to no avail.

Changing Lines

First Yin: Don't be wishy-washy, like the wind blowing through the leaves first one way, then the other. However, be obedient to your duty.

Second Yang: Don't be like a strong wind, blowing away the wheat with the chaff. This isn't the time to be stubborn.

Third Yang: You need advice and leadership, but be careful whom you listen to. Don't take bad advice, and avoid procrastination.

Fourth Yin: You can turn your subordinate position to your advantage if you think about it. Although you're in the weaker position, you can come out ahead. Even a gentle breeze is welcome on a hot day.

Fifth Yang: Make a strong effort to correct your faults before you make your next move. Fulfill your duty and you'll be noticed, but don't be a blowhard!

Sixth Yang: You're determined, but at this time you may be a bit susceptible to flattery and the influence of others. Don't be like a kite in the wind, controlled by another's hand. Someone may try to use this against you.

HEXAGRAM 58
Tui (Happiness)

The upper and lower trigrams are both Marsh, and Tui promises a time of joyous and productive *interaction* with others. Just as the marsh nourishes all plants and animals, so does Tui nourish the spirit of everyone with whom you come into contact. You can expect kindness from others, and in turn you must be kind to them.

Changing Lines

First Yang: Your outlook is good. Harmony is assured and there will be a minimum of friction.

Second Yang: Save your energy for important things and you'll be extremely fortunate. Concentrate on everyone's benefit.

Third Yin: Don't act in a contrived manner just to please others. Be honest about your feelings. Don't pretend to be satisfied if you're not.

Fourth Yang: You're happy with some things, displeased with others. This is because you're having trouble deciding between what you want to do and what you should do. The I Ching advises you to stick to the moral path.

Fifth Yang: You'll be all right unless you trust the wrong person. Don't trust everyone unquestioningly. You may want to keep your plans hidden even from your closest friends.

Sixth Yin: If you waste your energies trying to please everyone, you'll accomplish nothing. Act according to your nature.

HEXAGRAM 59
Huan (Scattering)

Huan, Water and Wind, shows departure and separation, although that which disperses will eventually be gathered together again. When wind blows across the water, there are ripples, so you'll probably be disturbed for a while until the ripples disperse.

Friends come together during certain times and then drift apart. Wounded relationships can be healed, and estranged loved ones can be reconciled. Just because there's separation now doesn't mean that this situation will last forever.

Changing Lines

First Yin: A new project or transition will leave you struggling to catch up, but once you establish your new routine, things will begin to flow for you. However, be obedient to your duty.

Second Yang: Important matters will require all your attention, so get yourself organized and then help others do the same. Help other people learn to fend for themselves.

Third Yin: There's danger brewing and you would be best served relocating. Seek your fortune elsewhere.

Fourth Yin: You've passed through a bad time, like metal through a forge. Your luck is about to improve. Your friends were there for you through the bad times, and they will help you celebrate the good times. Be on the lookout for new friends and relationships.

Fifth Yang: You have to be as strong as possible so that you'll set a good example for others. You might have to work through an illness or period of depression.

Sixth Yang: There's absolutely no reason to stay in a bad situation. Your karmic debt is paid through your own efforts. It's time to move on to better circumstances.

HEXAGRAM 60
Chieh (Limits)

Marsh and Water trigrams come together to signify self-control and awareness of your own limits. Sometimes we take on too much—too many responsibilities, the welfare of everyone around us, even situations that are beyond our control—and we wear ourselves out trying to take care of it all. We have to be realistic. Nobody can save the world by him- or herself, but we can do all we can (within reason) to make the world a better place.

Sometimes this hexagram warns us against overindulgence. We have to avoid overdoing food, drink, sex, or work.

Chieh also reminds us to be sensitive to other people's limitations. Don't expect more from other people then they are able to give. Recognize a person's level of competency and work well within his or her limits.

Changing Lines
First Yang: Your self-control will be tested by a new and challenging situation. Don't lose your temper; your example will be noticed by others.

Second Yang: Listen to your colleagues and don't resent advice given to you from well-meaning people. If you let your pride and stubbornness control your reactions, you'll lose the prize.

Third Yin: The keys to your happiness are in your hand. You have the power to change your life for the better if you're strong and brave. Be honest with yourself and avoid self-pity.

Fourth Yin: You might have to be strict with yourself for a time and avoid overindulgence. Practice restraint and learn to say "no"—especially to yourself!

Fifth Yang: You'll be able to accept the restrictions of your situation. After a while they'll become familiar and comfortable.

Sixth Yin: Life sometimes throws us a curve ball. There will be good times and bad times. Don't try to fight the way of nature. Each challenge helps reduce your karmic debt.

HEXAGRAM 61

Chung Fu (Confidence)

Here we find Marsh and Wind combined to represent a time of inner peace and *self-confidence*.

Now more than ever it is important to listen to your inner voice and follow your vision. There's no room for doubt or second-guessing. You must stride forward boldly and with great fanfare. A wonderful phase of your life awaits you and all you have to do is believe in yourself enough to meet it!

Changing Lines

First Yang: Trying a new approach is recommended as long as you think it through. Someone else may suggest this new idea, so listen carefully.

Second Yang: Your example will inspire others, and you'll be respected in circles of which you're totally unaware at the present time.

Third Yin: Sometimes when you follow your vision you have to do so by cooperating with others. Don't get impatient or demanding. Compromise is important, but don't sacrifice your ideals to satisfy other people.

Fourth Yin: It's good to leave untrustworthy companions. Even though you may miss them, you're better off without them. Your plans are about to come together and you can't allow anyone to deliberately undermine them.

Fifth Yang: Your friends may not always be the ones you need to ask for help. Sometimes you need the advice of an expert.

Sixth Yang: Be confident, but not overconfident. Don't aspire to heights for which you're unsuited. Gain experience first, find a firm footing, and then reach for the stars.

HEXAGRAM 62

Hsaio Kuo (Minor Problems)

Combining the trigrams for the Mountain and Thunder, Hsaio Kuo deals with minor problems. You're likely to get off to a few false starts and make a number of small mistakes, but these will be correctable. Your inner strength will be tested and through perseverance you'll find your way around these minor obstacles.

Temporary setbacks aren't always a waste of time. Our mistakes can be seen as learning experiences.

Changing Lines

First Yin: Fortune favors the prepared person. If you plan carefully, you'll amaze yourself at how well things work out for you. However, if you try to fly too high without proper precautions, you'll have a long way to fall.

Second Yin: Courtesy and politeness will get you further than stubbornness and arrogance. Interestingly enough, how you approach this time of your life is more important than winning your goal.

Third Yang: Luck is on your side for the moment, but don't get too cocky just yet. You're not completely out of danger yet.

Fourth Yang: Don't force yourself on others, and try not to make anyone jealous. This is a precarious time. Don't be too forceful or you'll encounter opposition; don't be too weak or you'll get left behind. Keep to the middle ground.

Fifth Yin: Your position is good but you may never advance beyond your present state. If you want to move ahead, you'll have to go somewhere else. If you're content where you are, no move is necessary.

Sixth Yin: You'll have to bend over backward to accommodate the demands of your situation. Be friendly, amiable, and patient even though nobody else shows you the same courtesy. You must rise above the limitations of human patience and take on the attributes of the Divine.

HEXAGRAM 63
Chi Chi (Finished)

Chi Chi combines Water and Fire. Since the Water is above the Fire, this is compared to the way fire and water cooperate to boil water. This can also be compared to how man and woman, though possessing different attributes and functions, can work together to form a relationship. In either case, Chi Chi means that the work is *finished*.

In its simplest manifestation, Chi Chi represents a phase of your life that has reached its peak. You've completed one cycle of your karmic work and another will begin soon. Take the lessons from this past phase and apply them toward the next level and you'll go even further.

Changing Lines

First Yang: Although you'll experience hindrances as you finish this phase, you'll struggle through to success. The closer you get to the prize, the more you'll feel like you're plodding through mud. Don't give up—persevere!

Second Yin: You'll have to let go of a few things to handle future challenges. Don't be afraid to sacrifice a little today to gain more tomorrow. Not only will you regain what you lost, you'll get even more in return.

Third Yang: Be strong and virtuous, both externally and in your inner attitudes. You'll have a lot of people cheering you on as you reach the finish line.

Fourth Yin: Be totally prepared for overlooked loose ends. Take them in stride and they'll pass quickly.

Fifth Yang: You're not completely finished yet, so don't slip into complacency or lazy habits. Stay focused and determined.

Sixth Yin: Be careful—your success could turn into failure if you make a wrong move. Take all the time you need to grow comfortable with your situation. You may have to help events settle into stability.

HEXAGRAM 64

Wei Chi (Not Finished)

Like Chi Chi, Wei Chi consists of Fire and Water, but reversed. Therefore the two elements are not yet in their correct places and can work against each other.

Due to this conflict, we can't assume that everything will work itself out. There's still chaos, confusion, and even danger, so we have to be like a fox crossing the water: alert, cautious, and careful not to get our tail wet.

Often Wei Chi means that you're in an antagonistic situation or relationship. No matter how hard you try, balance and harmony eludes you. If this is the case, you can't expect a perfect solution. There's going to be problems no matter what you do. The best solution is to practice patience, diplomacy, and compassion, and wait for the opportunity for a more balanced environment.

Wei Chi reminds us of the circular nature of existence. As soon as we finish one phase of our development, we enter another. This karmic dance never ends; it is forever and ever.

Changing Lines

First Yin: By all means, don't give anyone cause to criticize you. Your behavior must be impeccable. For this reason, you mustn't take on more than you can handle at this time. Finish all tasks with great diligence.

Second Yang: Keep walking along your current path, but be careful of hidden dangers. You're going to stumble a few times, but keep your eye on your destination and continue plodding along. You'll get there before you know it.

Third Yin: You're in a weak position to lead opposition, but be patient. Others may see you as weak if you don't push for action, but later on they'll realize that you were right all along. Try to avoid saying, "I told you so!"

Fourth Yang: The opportunity for which you've been waiting is arrived. This is the time to push forward. Fight for your rights; ask for what you deserve. If you don't like the situation, change it.

Fifth Yin: You have to be picky about whom you trust and with whom you work during this time. Associating with unreliable people will make your job much more difficult.

Sixth Yang: You'll enjoy success, but don't be boastful or it will be taken away. Don't let it go to your head. Remain calm and humble.

> *Fate is not an eagle, it creeps like a rat.*
>
> —Elizabeth Bowen, *The House in Paris*

AFTERWORD

Only the hand that erases can write the true thing.

—Meister Eckhart, *The Talks of Instruction*

*A*t this point we've reached the end of our exploration of the karmic aspects of the hand. May this book help you realize your own destiny and achieve the happiness and freedom that is your heritage as a child of the Universe.

I hope you've enjoyed this exploration of karma though the study of the palm. Some of the information may seem a little complex at first, but if I can figure it out, you certainly can too.

If this book has a theme, it would have to be that *through struggle we grow*. From a biological point of view, we are little different from our Stone Age ancestors. We thrive on challenge and adversity. Difficult as life may seem at times, without karmic challenges, our spirits stagnate. Whether you call this predisposition, fate, or karma, it all boils down to the same idea: we bring a task into this life, and in order to cleanse our souls we must first find this task and then undertake to complete it.

What we learn from all of this is karma's greatest lesson, one that seems to take us numerous lifetimes to grasp: that no matter what happens in life, we are ultimately struggling with nobody but ourselves. We are the source of and the solution to all our problems. We are the prison, and we alone have the key. I hope that this book helps you find the keys to your own karmic issues. May all the gods and goddesses bless you as you travel on your journey.

HOW I LEARNED KARMA FROM A CAT

You may have noticed that I dedicated this book to my cat Checkers, who died a few years ago. There's a very good reason for this, as everything I know about karma I learned from Checkers. The following is a tribute I wrote for the Feline CRF Information Center website. I hope you learn as much from this brave person as I did.

After fighting chronic renal failure for seven months and seven days, on October 27, 1998, our cat Checkers slipped into unconsciousness and had to be put to sleep. He was five and a half years old.

Checkers introduced himself to me five years ago when I was living in an apartment building in west Knoxville. I had just returned from going out for dinner with my son when a small black and white "tuxedo" kitten ran over to us, meowing loudly. I thought he probably belonged to one of the girls who lived downstairs. Although he shied away from letting me pet him, he followed us all the way to the door before returning to his perch on the front walk. He had a cocky way of walking with his head held high, as though he owned the place.

The next day, a bowl of dried cat food had appeared on the front walk, courtesy of the tenderhearted women on the bottom floor. The little kitten was guarding it, with his paws around the small bowl. He looked around proudly, glad of having such a prize. I was taken with the little rascal, and after a few inquiries, found out he was a stray. I thought if a bowl of cheap cat food made him so happy, he'd be delighted to have a house of his own to live in. I rubbed his head, and he let me. Later that day, he followed me into my apartment where he made himself at home. The deal was sealed. He knew an easy touch when he saw one.

From that day, my life became more interesting. One of the first things he did, once he thoroughly sniffed out my apartment, was break into one of the cupboards and pull out several bags of beans. That evening I came home to discover the kitchen floor covered with beans. Checkers managed to look both innocent and surprised, as though saying, "My goodness—how did that happen?" Some of my pots and pans were out too. I guess he wanted to make some chili.

He loved adventures. The day he returned from being neutered he managed to pull aside the seal around the air conditioner and I found him perched at the edge of the unit, swatting fearlessly at bats. My heart was in my throat because we lived on the second floor. He was still a bit groggy from anesthesia, and if he fell to the pavement, it would have killed him. We eventually persuaded him to come back in, and I carefully sealed the escape route.

Our dilemma was that Checkers couldn't stay at my apartment. The new landlord decreed that cats weren't allowed, even though he permitted dogs (I hope he's reincarnated as a mouse with a bad limp). However, Checkers and I had a plan. My girlfriend had a white cat named Oliver who used to get lonely and depressed when Elizabeth went out of town for work-related business. I introduced the two, and Checkers really laid on the charm. She fell in love with him, and he gave her his heart. Soon Oliver had a little brother to keep him company. Later Elizabeth and I were married and our family was complete.

Checkers was always absolutely fearless. This was never more apparent than when he became sick. His zest for life radiated from his spirit and never left him, even when he was close to the end. One time we came home and followed a trail of mayhem, which led to a twisted curtain rod that curved dramatically as it crossed the window. The curtains were in a tangled heap on the floor. The signs were unmistakable: Checkers had been here! He, of course, was calmly asleep on the bed.

He had escapist skills that would have rivaled Houdini's. Once Elizabeth called to tell me that Checkers had somehow gone outside. The bad news was that it was in the middle of one of the biggest blizzards in years. "How did he get out?" I asked. "He pried open the plumbing access panel and crawled along the pipes." I wasn't surprised; nothing he did could amaze me. She was able to eventually lure him out from under the neighbor's garage by offering him ham. He'd do just about anything for a piece of ham.

Checkers loved making difficult jumps to high places. He was a magician, splendid in his tuxedo. One morning I woke up and found him looking at me with his big yellow eyes from a precarious perch on top of the bedroom door. How he got there is a mystery that would baffle contemporary science. Once he jumped onto a drying rack and performed a parallel bar routine that would have won him Olympic gold. We never laughed so hard in our lives.

My son Jonathan constructed a "stronghold" from a cardboard box for Checkers, in which Checkers stashed his favorite toys. Sometimes Checkers would steal Oliver's toys and hide them in his box. I'd occasionally go through Checkers's stronghold and find little things that we had been missing.

Checkers was fascinated with bathroom activities and always escorted us to the privy. When we showered, he stood up on the glass and watched us. He also loved to ride around on my shoulder surveying his domain, and often he would reward me with a little kiss.

Checkers even tried to drink from straws. And whenever one of us went to the refrigerator, that vault full of sacred treats, he appeared and demanded a treat, which of course he always received.

I remember that he used to look behind paintings, convinced there were secret passageways behind them. Checkers was more than a pet—much more—he was a little person and a beloved member of our family, a part of everything we did. He was everywhere. Our house seems empty in a million places now that he's gone.

We first noticed he was sick in March. We were in the process of moving to a bigger house out in the country. With all the rooms and windows looking out into the woods, we knew that Checkers and Oliver would love it.

Checkers lost his appetite. We weren't worried at first because moving can be stressful to a cat, but when he completely refused to eat, we became concerned and took him to the vet. He had lost three pounds. His vet found traces of a synthetic fiber in his feces and thought he had an intestinal blockage. She treated Checkers with Laxatone and we took him home.

Two nights later he began vomiting and having mild convulsions. In a panic, we took him to a vet emergency hospital where the preliminary diagnosis was lymphatic cancer. We went home thinking he was going to die, while the clinic did tests on him. We didn't sleep that night as we waited for 6:00 A.M. to roll around.

When we picked him up in the morning, the emergency vet had bad news. He told us Checkers had advanced chronic renal failure and probably wouldn't live very long. His blood was saturated with two toxins—creatinine (a protein produced by muscle activity) and BUN (blood urea nitrogen)—both of which are usually filtered out by the kidneys. Checkers's kidneys were no longer able to do this job. X-rays showed that his kidneys had almost completely calcified, and the damage was irreversible. You can imagine our feelings. This was our introduction to the emotional roller coaster of CRF.

Checkers's regular vet was more optimistic and aggressively treated him with fluids and antibiotics. He responded, and we began to realize that Checkers wasn't going to die after all. However, he was going to need a lot of treatment and medications to keep him alive.

Since dehydration is a serious problem when the kidneys shut down, we learned how to give Checkers subcutaneous fluids. This involves sticking an IV needle into the skin between his shoulder blades and allowing fluids to run in under the skin. While this sounds traumatic, the parents' stress is far greater than the cat's. A cat's pain tolerance is much higher than ours, and after the first few times, we learned to insert the needle so well that Checkers didn't even feel it. It was much harder on us than it was on him. I almost fainted the first time I tried it.

Regular injections of Epogen and iron improved his anemia. We had to give him vitamins and bicarbonate of soda, both for gastritis and to help neutralize the acidity in his blood. Occasionally he required courses of antibiotics to fight infections.

Checkers made a dramatic comeback. For months he was like his normal self, although his creatinine and BUN were extremely high. The vet, who had made a specialty of CRF, kept a close watch on Checkers's condition and adapted his treatments as needed. He was back to his normal self, and he was full of energy. The worst part of the whole thing, as far as he was concerned, was sitting still for his subcutaneous fluids. We had our little boy back, and up went the roller coaster.

We hit our next valley in May. One morning we woke up and Checkers wasn't in bed with us. We found him in the guest room, hiding behind a stack of rugs. He was lethargic and vocalizing a piteous moaning sound. I said to Elizabeth, "I'm afraid he's dying," and we rushed him to the vet. She treated him with antibiotics and B-vitamin shots, and he snapped back almost immediately.

The problem with chronic renal failure (CRF) is that the cat has good days and bad days. They'll have "episodes" from which they rally for a while, until one day they don't rally. You can drive yourself crazy trying to interpret the cat's mood. It's frustrating and horrifying to watch someone you love die a little at a time and be unable to do anything about it. Cats can only communicate so much to you, and they're so stoic that they don't show symptoms until they're practically dead.

By now I had become obsessed with Checkers's condition, and I searched the web, visiting veterinary sites, downloading endless files, reading for hours everything I could find about CRF. I was searching for loopholes, for alternative treatments that might save Checkers's life. We considered a kidney transplant, but after reading about it, we decided the procedure and recovery would be too traumatic. Although his spirit and attitude were excellent, Checkers was a very sick cat and we were sure that he would never survive the operation. Finally, we had to accept that there was no magic answer, nothing that would give Checkers his kidneys back. All we could do was try to hold his illness at bay.

Checkers didn't care that his numbers were bad. All through the spring and summer he was cheerful and active. His coat sparkled and his big yellow eyes were full of fun and mischief. Because we knew he was on borrowed time, we showered him with love. His illness only made him even more special to us.

His positive attitude and love of life amazed us, considering he was dying of a terminal disease. Chalk it up to his will to live and his loving heart. One vet told me that in younger cats, it was better if the toxin levels increased gradually rather than suddenly spiking. Evidently a strong cat can gradually adapt to these levels over time.

A number of well-meaning people told us we should put Checkers to sleep rather than go through the time, money, and emotional trauma of treating a CRF cat. I believe that such folks do not realize that not all people walk on two legs. I feel sorry for them; they just don't understand what they're missing. Animals are the best people of all. This was never an option as long as Checkers could enjoy his life with good quality. We gladly did what we had to do—it was a small price for the time we bought.

The roller coaster ride recommenced that fall. As his disease slowly worsened, Checkers seemed to need more and more sleep, and one day he went into a serious decline. He suddenly became lethargic and semiconscious, showing no interest in his usual activities. We took him to the emergency clinic and after they did some bloodwork, we were told he wouldn't last the weekend.

Once again, we took him home (we thought) to die. We spent the entire long night with him, petting him and telling him we loved him. I decided to give him a special treat before he died, so I took him for a walk around the yard. He had never been outside before, because there are critters in the brush big enough to eat him. Yet now he was too sick to dart off into the woods. He carefully walked around the perimeter of the entire house, having a great time with the sights and smells, and often stopping to lie down and catch his breath. A squirrel taunted him from a tree and he glared back dire threats—the cat's version of shaking a fist. He ate a few bugs and some weeds, and I figured, *What the hell? Can't hurt him. You can't get any deader than dead.*

I was privileged to witness Checkers's finest moment. In front of the house, near the toolshed, he sniffed out a place where a couple of the neighborhood dogs mark their spot. He resolutely measured the boundaries of the mark and then performed the most magnificent act I've ever witnessed from anybody, human or feline. He turned around, lifted his tail rigidly erect, and with his lip curled in scorn, he *drenched* the dogs' area with the most copious shower of urine I've ever seen. He must have been storing it up, and he didn't miss a spot. This stream shot out a good eighteen inches and lasted several long seconds. I wish I could have seen the look on the dogs' faces when they found their special spot desecrated. If they could have found him, they probably would have killed him. I could almost hear Checkers think, *Stupid dogs.* This is how I'll always remember him, his finest moment.

Monday morning we took Checkers to his vet for what we thought would be some very bad news. But yet again he bounced back. He seemed to respond well to antibiotics, B-vitamin shots, and more aggressive fluid therapy. We were fortunate to have a vet who not only loved our cat, but was very informed about the disease.

By now we were trying to come up with a definite sign to tell us when it was time to put Checkers to sleep. We loved him too much to allow his condition to deteriorate to the final stage: convulsions and coma, and eventually death. The plan was this: when he lost interest in his food, we'd try him on tuna. When he lost interest in tuna, we knew it was time to let him go. Checkers loved to eat.

Checkers had begun losing interest in his special food for cats in renal failure, so I obtained another brand. He liked the new kind and his appetite improved, although he didn't gain very much weight back. He seemed like his old self again and we were ecstatic. He had a very good week.

It didn't last. Thursday night he had a seizure and once again slipped into lethargy. This episode was much worse than the previous ones; he didn't seem to recognize us and moaned every time he moved. We became badly scared when he wet the bed and didn't seem to notice. Helpless, we stayed up with him all night, trying to keep him comfortable and wondering if the time had come to finally let him go. The roller coaster had hit dead bottom.

This time the vet kept Checkers over the weekend to give him IV fluids. While he was there, Checkers made friends with a two-year-old jet-black stray the office had named Roy. We planned on bringing Roy home to be Checkers's and Oliver's brother, but decided to wait until Checkers was out of the woods first. We went in to see him every day to help with his fluids. When we picked him up on Monday, he was very glad to see us and seemed much better, although his creatinine and BUN hadn't significantly improved. He had come back yet again, and the roller coaster was on the upturn, although we knew in our hearts he didn't have much time.

Checkers had even less time than we thought. We took him home and he was in great spirits. He played with all of his toys, ate well from his own food bowl, used his own litter box, looked out of all his favorite windows, and seemed to feel fine. He did everything he loved to do; he missed nothing. Around six o'clock he seemed tired and went to bed, and I went with him to keep him company. I spent several hours with him, reading a book and petting him. He was always a very affectionate cat and Monday night he was especially so, pulling my hand close to his head and stroking my arm with his tail—something he had never done before. I thought this was because he was glad to be home. I think now that he somehow knew he didn't have much time left. I believe he was saying good-bye.

In the middle of the night I woke up and heard him getting a drink from the glass we kept on the bedside table. Then he used his litter box near the bed.

These normal sounds reassured me and I went back to sleep. The truly tragic part of this disease is that you rejoice whenever your cat does something normal.

The next morning he wasn't in bed with us, which was unusual. I searched all of his usual places for him, calling his name. He was in the last place I looked: the bottom of the closet. I had a premonition I would find him there, but I looked everywhere else first, hoping he was all right. I knew that if he was hiding in the closet, he was very, very ill.

Checkers was semiconscious. His eyes were unfocused, although he had periods when he would make eye contact with me. His tired eyes pleaded for us to do something to make him feel better. I offered him some tuna and he turned his head away. Elizabeth and I looked at each other. He had always trusted us to take care of him, and we knew it was time to let him go. There were not going to be any more good times. We had run out of ways to help him. We called the vet and made the arrangements.

We were offered the option to wait outside while they gave him the injection; we declined. We'd been with him through everything else thus far, and we weren't about to abandon him at the end. Everybody at the office loved him, and the vet and her assistant cried with us when they gave him the shot. I remember her telling him, "You're going to a better place Checkers; you're going to Heaven, and you'll never be sick again." I can't imagine that they weep for every cat they euthanize, but he was a very special little fellow. He became unconscious immediately and died peacefully without a sound. His little body, tensed with illness, relaxed, and with a sigh he slipped easily into the arms of death. We placed all his toys in his coffin with him, his favorite toy—an owl's feather—held between his paws. He looked like he was sleeping.

Checkers's battle was over. It wasn't his fault he couldn't go on any longer. He never gave up, but there were limits to what his spirit could make his failing body do. We buried him in our back yard with a funeral service surrounded by the people he loved the most. A week later we brought Roy home with us and renamed him Sam Boo.

Watching Checkers handle the progression of his disease with heroic spirit made me ashamed of my human weaknesses. A 240-pound man humbled by a 7-pound cat—there's gotta be a lesson in there somewhere (the smallest bodies often contain the largest spirits?). He's my hero.

Do we feel guilty about making the decision to put him to sleep? No. We did everything we could to provide the highest quality of life for Checkers as long as humanly possible. He told us very clearly that he was ready to go. Our house seems empty without him, and his brother Oliver misses him dreadfully. We're sad that we only got to have him with us for five years. We had looked forward to many, many more happy years with Checkers, and it was hard to let him go so young.

What caused his ravaging CRF is a mystery. The vet wondered if he had ingested something poisonous, but we couldn't think of what it could be. We found out that any infection that taxes a cat's immune system can damage the kidneys, and maybe that was the cause. Probably he just had a bad roll of the genetic dice and was born with faulty kidneys—we'll never know.

Throughout his illness, we blamed ourselves. We tormented ourselves trying to figure out what we could have done differently. Did we leave a cleaning chemical out? Were we lax on visits to the vet? Were there symptoms that we were too preoccupied with other things to recognize? Looking back on it, we know we didn't do anything wrong. There was no way to recognize his illness and even his vet, who is really good, missed it at first. Nor could we have prevented it from happening even if we had recognized it earlier.

Nobody with a terminally ill cat should feel guilty or responsible for their cat's condition. There simply wasn't anything else we could have done, and this is the horrible and frustrating truth. He was probably sick a long time before he actually showed any symptoms, but this is a cat who, the day before he died, was playing with his favorite owl feather and taking great pains to show his mom and his dad how much he loved us. He refused to acknowledge his illness until it was killing him.

I believe that the amount of love Checkers received and returned contributed to his good attitude and dramatic recoveries. Love is an essential component of an energy circuit that flows around us and powers life. Even CRF, though it ravaged his body, couldn't overcome the strength of his loving spirit. He knew a thousand ways to show us his love. Stupid humans—we only knew a few ways to show ours, but I think he forgave us our limitations. Excruciating as it was, putting him to sleep was the last loving act we could do for him. I'm convinced of that now.

Checkers has crossed the Rainbow Bridge and is having a great time, snacking on whatever he wants and chasing ghostly mice all over the place. Yet now and again, out of the corner of my eye, I see a little black-and-white cat leaping about, and I think perhaps he's stopping by to check on us. When I turn to look, he's gone. He has a lot to do, and Heaven is a big place.

Checkers taught me that love doesn't end just because the body does. We will never forget him.

Flow with whatever happens and let your mind be free.

Stay centered by accepting whatever you are doing.

This is the best Way.

—Chuang Tsu, *Inner Chapters*

BIBLIOGRAPHY & SUGGESTED READING

Blechsmidt, E. *The Stages of Human Development before Birth*. London: W. B. Saunders, 1961.

Brennan, J. H. *The Magical I Ching*. St. Paul, Minn.: Llewellyn Publications, 2000.

Bright, Jagat S. *The Dictionary of Palmistry*. New York: Bell Publishing Company, 1958.

Cheiro. *The Language of the Hand*. Chicago: Rand McNally & Co., 1900.

———. *Palmistry for All*. London: G. P. Putnam & Sons, 1916.

Chuang Tsu. *Inner Chapters*. Translated by Gia-Fu-Feng and Jane English. New York: Random House, 1974.

Collinger, William. *The American Holistic Health Association Complete Guide to Alternative Medicine*. New York: Warner Books, 1996.

Das, S. K. *Everybody's Guide to Palmistry*. New Delhi, India: Sterling Publishers Ltd., 1986.

Davies, Oliver, trans. *Meister Eckhart: Selected Writings*. New York: Penguin Books, 1994.

Dukes, Terrence. *Chinese Hand Analysis*. York Beach, Maine: Samuel Weiser, Inc., 1987.

Fox, Judy, Karen Hughes, and John Tampion. *An Illuminated I Ching*. New York: Arco Publishing Company, 1984.

Gettings, Fred. *The Book of the Hand*. London: Triune Books, 1974.

Ho, Kwok Man, Martin Palmer, and Joanne O'Brien. *Lines of Destiny*. Boston: Shambala Press, 1986.

Karges, Craig, and Jon Saint-Germain. *The Wizard's Legacy: A Tale of Real Magic*. Washington, D.C.: Leading Authorities Press, 2002.

Legge, James. *The I Ching or the Book of Changes*. New York: Dover Publications, 1963.

Rao, R. G. *Your Destiny in Thumb*. 2d ed. New Delhi, India: Ranjan Publications, 1983.

Ritsema, Rudolf, and Stephen Karcher. *I Ching: The Classic Oracle of Change*. New York: Barnes and Noble, 1995.

Scheimann, Eugene, M.D. *A Doctor's Guide to Better Health Through Palmistry*. New York: Parker Publishing Company, 1969.

Spier, Julius. *The Hands of Children*. 2d ed. London: Routledge & Kegan Paul Ltd., 1955.

Walpole, Rahula. *What the Buddha Taught*. 2d ed. New York: Grove Press, Inc., 1974.

Webster, Richard. *Soul Mates*. St. Paul, Minn.: Llewellyn Publications, 2001.

Wilhelm, Richard, and Cary F. Baynes. *The I Ching or Book of Changes*. Princeton, N.J.: Princeton University Press, 1967.

INDEX

Runic Palmistry

JON SAINT-GERMAIN

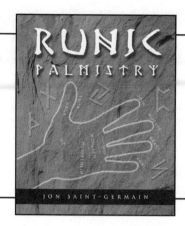

This unique book combines standard palmistry, Norse mythology, and the runes, using all three to understand a person and his or her path, personality, needs, and special gifts.

It is a system handed down orally through four generations of Jon Saint-Germain's family, originally learned from a mysterious Scandinavian who entered the family circle two hundred years ago. In this system, lines of the palm are called "branches," and mounts of the palm are named after Norse deities. You will learn the meanings of the fingers in the light of exciting Norse mythology. This is the only book on the subject available.

- Easily learn and remember the meanings of the lines and mounts of the palm through a lively presentation of Norse names and mythology
- Discover the meaning of the twenty-four runic symbols, how to construct your own set of runes, and how to handle them to respect their energies
- Combine palm reading with a rune cast to provide a complete picture of someone's past, present, and future
- Find runic symbols within the palm and discover how to tell which ones are active at any given time in a person's life

1-56718-577-0
240 pp., 7½ x 9⅛

$14.95

To order, call 1-877-NEW-WRLD
Prices subject to change without notice

Palm Reading for Beginners
Find the Future in the Palm of Your Hand

RICHARD WEBSTER

Announce in any gathering that you read palms and you will be flocked by people thrilled to show you their hands. When you are have finished *Palm Reading for Beginners*, you will be able to look at anyone's palm (including your own) and confidently and effectively tell them about their personality, love life, hidden talents, career options, prosperity, and health.

Palmistry is possibly the oldest of the occult sciences, with basic principles that have not changed in 2,600 years. This step-by-step guide clearly explains the basics, as well as advanced research conducted in the past few years on such subjects as dermatoglyphics.

Now you can learn to read palms even if you have no prior knowledge of the subject.

1-56718-791-9
264 pp., 5³⁄₁₆ x 8, illus. $9.95

Spanish edition:
Quiromancia para principiantes
0-7387-0396-6 $10.95

Instant Palm Reader
A Road Map to Life

LINDA DOMIN

Etched upon your palm is an aerial view of all the scenes you will travel in the course of your lifetime. Your characteristics, skills, and abilities are imprinted in your mind and transferred as images on to your hand. Now, with this simple, flip-through pictorial guide, you can assemble your own personal palm reading, like a professional, almost instantly.

The *Instant Palm Reader* shows you how your hands contain the picture of the real you—physically, emotionally, and mentally. More than 500 easy-to-read diagrams will provide you with candid, uplifting revelations about yourself: personality, childhood, career, finances, family, love life, talents, and destiny.

With the sensitive information artfully contained within each interpretation, you will also be able to uncover your hidden feelings and unconscious needs as you learn the secrets of this 3,000-year-old science.

1-56718-232-1
256 pp., 7 x 10, illus.   **$14.95**

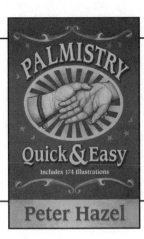

Palmistry Quick & Easy

PETER HAZEL

Gain instant access to this ancient science. *Palmistry Quick & Easy* brings New Millennium awareness and interpretations to centuries of traditional knowledge of palmistry. The innovative interactive format leads you through 232 different questions and 170 illustrations designed to give you perceptive insight into the deepest motivations of yourself and others.

Experienced palmists will also find this book to be a useful and concise reference, neatly divided into the traditional categories: length of the palm and fingers, the four hand types, thumbs, marks on fingers, the lines, fingernails, the mounts, timing in the palm, and even the meaning of rings.

- Features an innovative interactive format with 170 palm illustrations
- Contains topics not included in most other palmistry books: notes for astrologers, parents, personnel managers, lovers, and marriage counselors
- Includes an intriguing treatment of the Chinese view of hands, a view of traditional hands, and the Wiccan view of hands
- Follow easy guidelines for reflexology, or massaging the hand for relaxation and removing blocks

1-56718-410-3
240 pp., 5³⁄₁₆ x 8, 170 illus. $9.95

How to Uncover Your Past Lives

TED ANDREWS

Knowledge of your past lives can be extremely rewarding. It can assist you in opening to new depths within your own psychological makeup. It can provide greater insight into present circumstances with loved ones, career, and health. It is also a lot of fun.

Now Ted Andrews shares with you nine different techniques that you can use to access your past lives. Between techniques, Andrews discusses issues such as karma and how it is expressed in your present life, the source of past life information, soul mates and twin souls, proving past lives, the mysteries of birth and death, animals and reincarnation, abortion and premature death, and the role of reincarnation in Christianity.

To explore your past lives, you need only use one or more of the techniques offered. Complete instructions are provided for a safe and easy regression. Learn to dowse to pinpoint the years and places of your lives with great accuracy, make your own self-hypnosis tape, attune to the incoming child during pregnancy, use the tarot and the cabala in past life meditations, keep a past life journal, and more.

0-87542-022-2
224 pp., mass market, illus.   **$5.99**

Spanish edition:
Cómo descubrir sus vidas pasadas
1-56718-028-0   **$9.95**

To order, call 1-877-NEW-WRLD
Prices subject to change without notice

Practical Guide to Past-Life Memories
Twelve Proven Methods

RICHARD WEBSTER

Past life memories can provide valuable clues as to why we behave the way we do. They can shed light on our purpose in life, and they can help us heal our current wounds. Now you can recall your past lives on your own, without the aid of a hypnotist.

This book includes only the most successful and beneficial methods used in the author's classes. Since one method does not work for everyone, you can experiment with twelve different straightforward techniques to find the best one for you.

This book also answers many questions, such as "Do I have a soul mate?", "Does everyone have a past life?", "Is it dangerous?", and "What about déjà vu?"

- No other book covers as many methods for recalling past lives
- For the first time in print: how to return to a previous incarnation with your spirit guide
- Filled with case studies that illustrate each method
- Features only the most successful methods from the author's own classes

0-7387-0077-0
264 pp., 5³⁄₁₆ x 8 $9.95

Spanish edition:
Regrese a sus vidas pasadas
0-7387-0196-3 $12.95

To order, call 1-877-NEW-WRLD
Prices subject to change without notice

Soul Mates
Understanding Relationships
Across Time

RICHARD WEBSTER

The eternal question: how do you find your soul mate—that special, magical person with whom you have spent many previous incarnations? Popular metaphysical author Richard Webster explores every aspect of the soul mate phenomenon in his newest release.

The incredible soul mate connection allows you and your partner to progress even further with your souls' growth and development with each incarnation. *Soul Mates* begins by explaining reincarnation, karma, and the soul, and prepares you to attract your soul mate to you. After reading examples of soul mates from the author's own practice, and famous soul mates from history, you will learn how to recall your past lives. In addition, you will gain valuable tips on how to strengthen your relationship so it grows stronger and better as time goes by.

1-56718-789-7
240 pp., 6 x 9 $12.95

Spanish edition:
Almas gemelas
0-7387-0063-0 $12.95

To order, call 1-877-NEW-WRLD
Prices subject to change without notice

Journey of Souls
Case Studies of Life Between Lives

MICHAEL NEWTON, PH.D.

This remarkable book uncovers—for the first time—the mystery of life in the spirit world after death on earth. Dr. Michael Newton, a hypnotherapist in private practice, has developed his own hypnosis technique to reach his subjects' hidden memories of the hereafter. The narrative is woven as a progressive travel log around the accounts of twenty-nine people who were placed in a state of superconsciousness. While in deep hypnosis, these subjects describe what has happened to them between their former reincarnations on earth. They reveal graphic details about how it feels to die, who meets us right after death, what the spirit world is really like, where we go and what we do as souls, and why we choose to come back in certain bodies.

After reading *Journey of Souls*, you will acquire a better understanding of the immortality of the human soul. Plus, you will meet day-to-day personal challenges with a greater sense of purpose as you begin to understand the reasons behind events in your own life.

1-56718-485-5
288 pp., 6 x 9 $14.95

TO WRITE TO THE AUTHOR

If you wish to contact the author or would like more information about this book, please write to the author in care of Llewellyn Worldwide and we will forward your request. Both the author and publisher appreciate hearing from you and learning of your enjoyment of this book and how it has helped you. Llewellyn Worldwide cannot guarantee that every letter written to the author can be answered, but all will be forwarded. Please write to:

Jon Saint-Germain
℅ Llewellyn Worldwide
P.O. Box 64383, Dept. 0-7387-0317-6
St. Paul, MN 55164-0383, U.S.A.

Please enclose a self-addressed stamped envelope for reply,
or $1.00 to cover costs. If outside U.S.A., enclose
international postal reply coupon.

Many of Llewellyn's authors have websites with additional information and resources. For more information, please visit our website at:

http://www.llewellyn.com